HOW TO MAKE MILLIONS FROM YOUTUBE

Turbocharge Your Channel and Transform it into a Profitable Money-Making Machine

HAMZA MUNIR

Copyright © 2023 by HAMZA MUNIR

All rights reserved.

Contents

Introduction	1
Part I	4
1. Introduction to Making Money on YouTube	5
2. Understanding the YouTube Platform	11
3. Choosing Your Niche and Target Audience	17
4. Exploring Different YouTuber Categories	23
5. Setting Up Your YouTube Channel	35
6. Creating High-Quality Content	41
7. Building Your Subscriber Base	48
8. Optimizing Video Titles, Descriptions, and Tags	54
9. Utilizing Thumbnails and Video Graphics	60
Part II	66
10. Joining the YouTube Partner Program	67
11. Understanding Ad Revenue and CPM	74
12. Exploring Alternative Revenue Streams	80
13. Sponsorships and Brand Collaborations	86

14.	Affiliate Marketing on YouTube	92
15.	Merchandise and Product Sale	98

Part III — 104

16.	Engaging with Your Audience	105
17.	Utilizing Social Media to Promote Your Channel	109
18.	Cross-Promotion and Collaboration Strategies	118
19.	YouTube SEO and Algorithm Optimization	123
20.	Analyzing Analytics and Insights	129
21.	Understanding Trending Topics and Viral Content	134

Part IV — 139

22.	Developing a Content Strategy	140
23.	Expanding Your YouTube Presence	145
24.	Internationalizing Your Channel	150
25.	Scaling Your Channel with a Team	157
26.	Creating Evergreen Content	165
27.	Building Your Personal Brand	171

Part V — 177

28.	Time Management and Productivity Tips	178
29.	Managing Finances and Taxes	184
30.	Protecting Your Intellectual Property	189
31.	Dealing with Copyright Issues	195
32.	Handling Controversies and Negative Feedback	200

33.	Expanding Your Online Presence Beyond YouTube	206
Part VI		213
34.	Creating and Selling Digital Products	214
35.	Writing Books and Publishing eBooks	222
36.	Public Speaking and Hosting Events	229
37.	Licensing and Syndication Opportunities	234
38.	Investing and Growing Your Wealth	241
Part VII		248
39.	Keeping Up with YouTube Policies and Guidelines	249
40.	Understanding YouTube Algorithm Updates	257
41.	How Much YouTube Pay for ONE Million views?	265
42.	The Final Stretch: Wishing You Millions on Your YouTube Journey	270
About the Author		273

Introduction

Are you ready to unlock the untapped potential of YouTube and turn your passion into a profitable venture? Look no further! "How to Make Millions from YouTube: A Comprehensive Guide" is your ultimate roadmap to navigating the exciting world of YouTube and transforming your channel into a lucrative business.

In this digital era, YouTube has emerged as a powerhouse for content creators, providing countless opportunities to connect with millions of viewers around the globe. With over 2 billion logged-in monthly active users and over 500 hours of video content uploaded every minute, YouTube has become a platform where creativity and entrepreneurship intersect. However, with such a vast sea of content, it can be overwhelming to stand out and monetize your efforts effectively. That's where this book comes in.

"How to Make Millions from YouTube: A Comprehensive Guide" is designed to be your trusted companion on your journey to YouTube success. This book goes beyond the basics of creating and uploading videos; it delves deep into the strategies, techniques, and insider knowledge that can help you not only build an engaged audience but also generate substantial income from your YouTube channel.

Whether you're an aspiring YouTuber or an established creator looking to take your channel to new heights, this guide offers a comprehensive blueprint for success. From understanding the YouTube ecosystem to leveraging analytics, optimizing your videos, and exploring different monetization methods, every aspect of building a thriving YouTube channel is covered in detail.

We examine YouTube's foundations in the first section of the book, outlining its history, its influence on the media ecosystem, and the options it offers content providers. You'll gain a solid understanding of the YouTube algorithm, discover the different types of content that thrive on the platform, and learn how to identify your niche and target audience.

Next, we explore the strategies for creating high-quality, engaging content that captures viewers' attention and keeps them coming back for more. You'll learn the art of storytelling, how to develop a unique brand identity, and the importance of consistent branding across your channel. We'll also delve into the technical aspects of video production, offering tips on filming, editing, and optimizing your videos for maximum impact.

Once you have compelling content, it's time to grow your audience and increase your channel's visibility. This guide provides you with proven techniques to boost your channel's discoverability through effective search engine optimization (SEO), social media promotion, collaborations, and cross-promotion strategies. We'll also cover the power of analytics and how to leverage the data to make informed decisions and optimize your content strategy.

Of course, no YouTube success story is complete without addressing the various monetization methods available to creators. In this book, we explore the different ways you can make money from your YouTube channel, including advertising revenue, brand partnerships, merchandise sales, crowdfunding, and more. We'll guide you through the process of setting up and optimizing your YouTube monetization options to maximize your earnings potential.

Whether you dream of becoming a full-time YouTuber, generating passive income, or simply sharing your passion with the world while making some extra cash, "How to Make Millions from YouTube: A Comprehensive Guide" is your essential resource. It empowers you to unlock the untapped potential of YouTube, cultivate a dedicated audience, and transform your channel into a lucrative business. Get ready to embark on an exciting and rewarding adventure in the world of YouTube!

Part I
Getting Started with YouTube

Chapter 1

Introduction to Making Money on YouTube

WELCOME TO THE EXCITING world of YouTube, where millions of creators have turned their passion into profitable careers. In this chapter, we will dive into the fundamentals of making money on YouTube and explore the various opportunities that await you. Whether you are an aspiring content creator or an entrepreneur looking to leverage the power of this platform, get ready to unlock the secrets to success and learn how to make millions from YouTube.

Understanding the YouTube Landscape

Before we delve into the strategies and techniques for monetizing your YouTube channel, it is important to understand the platform and its immense potential. YouTube is the world's largest video-sharing platform, with over 2 billion logged-in monthly users consuming billions of hours of content. It's also a great way to make money. In fact, some YouTubers make millions of dollars each year.

This presents an incredible opportunity for creators to reach a vast global audience and generate substantial income.

Building a Strong Foundation

To make money on YouTube, you need to build a strong foundation for your channel. This involves identifying your niche, defining your target audience, and creating high-quality content that captivates and engages viewers. Your content should be unique, valuable, and aligned with your viewers' interests. Remember, consistency is key. Regularly uploading content builds your channel's authority and keeps your audience coming back for more.

Maximising Revenue and Growth

SEO and Video Optimization: Search Engine Optimization (SEO) plays a crucial role in increasing your channel's visibility and attracting organic traffic. Perform thorough keyword research to gain insight into the search queries of your target audience, allowing you to optimize your video titles, descriptions, and tags effectively. Engaging thumbnails and compelling video descriptions can also help improve click-through rates and viewer engagement.

Collaboration and Cross-Promotion:

Collaborating with other YouTubers in your niche can expand your reach and expose your channel to new audiences. Look for creators who share a similar target audience but offer complementary content. Collaborative videos and cross-promotion on each other's channels an drive traffic, increase subscribers, and open doors to potential sponsorship opportunities.

Audience Engagement and Community Building:

Building a strong relationship with your viewers is vital for long-term success. Actively engage with your audience by responding to comments, hosting live streams, and conducting Q&A sessions. Foster a sense of community by encouraging discussions, showcasing user-generated content, and involving your viewers in your creative process. A loyal and engaged audience is more likely to support you financially and spread the word about your channel.

Diversifying Your Revenue Streams:

While ad revenue is an essential part of monetizing your YouTube channel, it is wise to diversify your income streams. Explore additional avenues such as affiliate marketing, online courses, e-books, and brand collaborations outside of YouTube. By diversifying your revenue streams, you can decrease dependence on a single source of income and unlock greater earning potential.

Adapting to Changes and Evolving Strategies:

The landscape of YouTube is ever-changing, with algorithm updates, policy revisions, and shifts in viewer preferences. Remaining well-informed and adapting your strategies accordingly is of utmost importance.

Continuously analyze your channel's performance, track viewer analytics, and experiment with different content formats to understand what resonates best with your audience. Embrace innovation, stay ahead of the curve, and be willing to evolve as the platform evolves.

If you're thinking about starting a YouTube channel, you're probably wondering how you can make money from it. Here are some things you must need to know:

You need to have a lot of views. The more views your videos get, the more money you'll make.

You need to have a lot of subscribers. Subscribers are invaluable individuals who have made the conscious decision to follow your channel. The greater the number of subscribers you accumulate, the higher the likelihood that your videos will be seen by a wider audience.

You need to have good content. Your videos need to be interesting and engaging. If people don't enjoy watching your videos, they're not going to watch them again.

If you can do all of these things, you'll be well on your way to making money from YouTube.

How to Make Money from YouTube?

There are a few ways to make money from YouTube.

Google AdSense. It is the most common and important way to make money from YouTube. When you sign up for AdSense, you'll place ads on your videos. When people watch your videos and click on the ads, you'll earn money.

Channel memberships. This is an emerging avenue for generating revenue through YouTube. Channel members pay a monthly fee to get access to exclusive content, such as behind-the-scenes videos, live streams, and merchandise discounts.

Product sales. You can also generate income from YouTube by establishing a revenue stream through product sales. You can promote your products in your videos, in your channel descriptions, and in your social media posts.

Making Money from YouTube is Possible

Making money from YouTube is possible, but it takes hard work and dedication. If you're willing to put in the effort, you can earn a good living from your YouTube channel.

Here are some valuable tips to help you get started:

Choose a niche. What are you passionate about? What do you know a lot about? Choose a niche that you're interested in and that you know you can talk about for hours.

Create high-quality videos. This means using good equipment, editing your videos well, and creating content that is interesting and engaging.

Promote your videos. Share them on social media, submit them to video sharing websites, and reach out to other YouTubers who might be interested in collaborating.

Be patient. Building a successful YouTube channel takes time and dedication. It's important to set realistic expectations and understand that substantial monetary gains may not happen overnight. Just keep creating great content and promoting your channel, and eventually you'll start to see results.

Making money on YouTube is not a quick path to overnight success. It requires dedication, consistency, and a deep understanding of your audience and the platform. By building a strong foundation, leveraging the YouTube Partner Program, exploring diverse monetization strategies, and nurturing your audience, you can turn your YouTube channel into a lucrative business venture. Remember to stay authentic, create valuable content, and adapt to changes as you embark on this exciting journey to make millions from YouTube.

Now that you have gained a solid introduction to making money on YouTube, it's time to delve deeper into the strategies, techniques, and insider secrets that will propel you towards success. In the upcoming chapters, we will explore each monetization method in detail, provide actionable tips and case studies, and guide you towards building a thriving YouTube empire. Get ready to unlock your potential and make your mark in the world of online content creation.

Chapter 2

Understanding the YouTube Platform

UNDERSTANDING THE YOUTUBE PLATFORM

In this chapter, we will dive deep into understanding the YouTube platform, its inner workings, and the key elements that contribute to your success as a content creator. By gaining a comprehensive understanding of the platform, you will be able to optimize your content, engage your audience effectively, and unlock the full potential of YouTube to generate substantial revenue.

The Power of YouTube:

YouTube has revolutionized the way we consume video content. With over 2 billion monthly active users and an ever-growing community, it has become the go-to platform for entertainment, education, and self-expression. It offers a global stage where creators can share their talents, expertise, and passions with the world.

Creating a YouTube Channel:

Before diving into the intricacies of the platform, let's start with the basics: creating your YouTube channel. Setting up a channel is a straightforward process. Simply sign in with your Google account, choose a channel name, customize your channel art and logo, and you're ready to go. Your channel is your online identity, so make sure to create a visually appealing and professional brand image.

Navigating the Creator Studio

Once your channel is up and running, it's time to familiarize yourself with the Creator Studio. This is your control center, where you can manage and optimize your content. The Creator Studio allows you to upload videos, analyze performance metrics, engage with your audience through comments, and monetize your content.

Content Strategy and Planning

To succeed on YouTube, you need a well-defined content strategy. Understanding your target audience and their interests is crucial. Research popular topics and trends in your niche, and brainstorm ideas that will captivate and engage your viewers. Create a content calendar to ensure consistency and plan your videos in advance.

Engaging Video Production

Creating high-quality videos is essential to capturing your audience's attention and keeping them engaged. Invest in good equipment, such as cameras, microphones, and lighting, to enhance the production value of your content. Pay attention to audio quality, as it is often overlooked but plays a significant role in viewer satisfaction. Edit your videos meticulously to maintain a professional standard.

Building an Engaged Community

One of the key strengths of YouTube is its community aspect. Foster a sense of community by actively engaging with your viewers. Respond to comments, ask for feedback, and encourage discussions. Show genuine interest in your audience's opinions and create a positive and inclusive environment. This not only builds loyalty but also increases the likelihood of your videos being shared and recommended.

Leveraging Social Media

Promoting your YouTube channel on social media platforms can significantly boost your reach and attract new viewers. Create accounts on popular social media platforms such as Instagram, Twitter, and Facebook, and regularly share teasers, behind-the-scenes content, and updates about your latest videos. Engage with your followers and collaborate with other creators to expand your network.

Analytics and Performance Tracking

Understanding the performance of your videos is crucial for optimizing your content and making informed decisions. YouTube provides robust analytics tools that give you insights into your channel's performance, audience demographics, watch time, engagement, and more. Regularly analyze these metrics to identify trends, patterns, and areas for improvement. Use this data to refine your content strategy and tailor your videos to better resonate with your audience.

Collaboration and Cross-Promotion

Collaborating with other YouTubers can be mutually beneficial and help expand your reach. Seek out creators in your niche with a similar audience and propose collaboration ideas. This can involve creating videos together, featuring each other in your content, or cross-promoting each other's channels. Collaborations introduce your channel to a new audience and can lead to increased subscribers and viewership.

Staying Consistent and Adapting

Consistency is key on YouTube. Regularly upload videos according to your content calendar and maintain a consistent brand image. By consistently delivering valuable content, you build trust and loyalty with your audience. However, it's also important to stay adaptable and evolve with changing trends and audience preferences. Pay attention to viewer feedback, experiment with new video formats, and stay updated with the latest YouTube features and policies.

Copyright and Fair Use

Respecting copyright laws and understanding fair use is essential to avoid potential legal issues on YouTube. Ensure that you have the necessary rights to use any copyrighted material, such as music, images, or clips, in your videos. Familiarize yourself with YouTube's policies regarding copyright infringement and fair use, and always give proper credit when using third-party content.

Dealing with Challenges and Criticism

As a content creator on YouTube, you may encounter challenges and criticism along the way. It's important to develop a thick skin and handle negativity in a constructive manner. Embrace feedback and use it as an opportunity to improve. Engage in healthy discussions with your audience but avoid getting involved in online disputes or responding to trolls. Focus on creating quality content and nurturing your loyal viewers.

YouTube Algorithm and Trend Surfing

Understanding how the YouTube algorithm works can give you an edge in maximizing your video's visibility. While the exact algorithm remains a closely guarded secret, there are certain factors that can influence video rankings, such as watch time, engagement, and viewer retention. Stay informed about algorithm updates and trends, and adapt your content strategy accordingly. Trend surfing can help you ride the wave of popular topics and attract more viewers to your channel.

Managing Your Channel's Growth

As your channel grows, it's important to manage your success effectively. Delegate tasks if necessary, such as editing or social media management, to maintain consistency and quality. Consider hiring a team or collaborating with freelancers to scale your operations. Keep track of your revenue and expenses, and invest wisely in equipment, marketing, and further professional development.

Understanding the YouTube platform is the foundation for your success as a content creator. By grasping the intricacies of the platform, optimizing your content, engaging with your audience, and leveraging monetization options, you can unlock the true potential of YouTube and turn your passion into a profitable venture. Remember to stay committed, adapt to changes, and always strive for continuous improvement. With dedication and the right strategies, you can achieve your goals and make millions from YouTube.

Chapter 3

Choosing Your Niche and Target Audience

IN THIS CHAPTER, WE will delve into the crucial process of choosing your niche and target audience on YouTube. Selecting the right niche and identifying your target audience are fundamental steps towards building a successful YouTube channel that can generate substantial income. This chapter will guide you through the process of discovering your niche, understanding your target audience, and positioning yourself for maximum growth and profitability.

Uncover Your Passion and Expertise

The first step in choosing your niche is to identify your passion and expertise. Ask yourself: What subjects or topics do I genuinely enjoy? What am I knowledgeable about? It's crucial to choose a niche that you are passionate about because this enthusiasm will be reflected in your content and resonate with your audience. Remember, viewers can sense authenticity, and your passion will help you establish credibility and attract loyal followers.

Research Popular and Profitable Niches

While passion is essential, it's also vital to consider the popularity and profitability of different niches. Conduct thorough research to identify niches that have a substantial following and offer opportunities for monetization. Look for niches that have a dedicated audience, consistent demand, and potential for collaboration with brands. Explore YouTube's trending videos, review popular channels, and use keyword research tools to discover niche ideas that align with your interests and have market potential.

Narrow Down Your Niche

Once you have a list of potential niches, it's time to narrow down your options. Consider the level of competition within each niche and evaluate your unique angle or perspective. Aim for a niche that strikes a balance between popularity and competition, allowing you to carve out a distinct presence. For example, instead of a broad fitness channel, you could focus on a niche like high-intensity interval training for busy professionals. The more specific your niche, the easier it will be to target your audience and establish yourself as an expert.

Understand Your Target Audience

To create content that appeals to them and encourages participation, it is imperative to comprehend your target audience. Establish the characteristics of your target audience, like their age, gender, geography, and interests, to start. Use YouTube analytics and social media insights to gain valuable data about your existing audience or conduct surveys and interviews to gather more information. This knowledge will help you tailor your content, language, and overall approach to appeal directly to your ideal viewers.

Identify Audience Needs and Pain Points

To truly connect with your target audience, you need to identify their needs, challenges, and pain points. What problems are they facing? What information or entertainment are they seeking? Conduct market research, engage with your audience through comments and messages, and analyze competitor channels to gain insights into the gaps you can fill. By addressing your audience's specific needs, you can position yourself as a valuable resource and build a loyal following.

Differentiate Yourself

In a sea of YouTube channels, it's crucial to differentiate yourself from the competition. Analyze other channels in your niche and identify what makes them successful and unique. Then, find your own voice and USP (Unique Selling Proposition). Showcase your personality, expertise, or storytelling skills in a way that sets you apart. Remember, authenticity is key, and viewers are more likely to connect with genuine personalities. Stay true to yourself while leveraging your strengths to stand out in your chosen niche.

Test and Refine:

Choosing a niche and target audience is not a one-time decision; it's an iterative process. As you start creating content and engaging with your audience, be open to feedback and data-driven insights. Monitor your YouTube analytics, pay attention to comments and messages, and adapt accordingly. Experiment with different formats, styles, and topics to find what resonates best with your audience. This testing phase will help you refine your content strategy and further narrow down your target audience.

Collaborate and Network:

Building a successful YouTube channel is not a solitary endeavor. Collaborating with other creators in your niche can help you expand your reach, gain exposure to new audiences, and build valuable connections. Look for opportunities to collaborate on videos, podcasts, or live streams with creators who share a similar target audience or complementary content. Networking within your niche can also open doors to sponsorships, brand partnerships, and cross-promotion, further enhancing your channel's growth and revenue potential.

Adapt to Market Trends:

The digital landscape, including YouTube, is constantly evolving. To stay relevant and maintain your competitive edge, it's crucial to adapt to market trends. Keep a close eye on emerging topics, viral content, and shifts in audience preferences. Stay informed about algorithm updates and changes in YouTube policies to optimize your content strategy. Being proactive and adaptable will help you remain at the forefront of your niche and continue to attract and retain viewers.

Stay Engaged with Your Audience:

One of the keys to building a loyal and engaged audience is maintaining consistent interaction and engagement. Respond to comments, address viewer questions, and participate in community discussions. Show appreciation for your viewers' support and feedback. Regularly seek input from your audience through polls, surveys, and Q&A sessions to understand their evolving interests and preferences. By fostering a sense of community and actively involving your audience, you'll create a dedicated following that will eagerly anticipate your content and contribute to your channel's success.

Choosing the right niche and target audience is a critical foundation for your YouTube channel's success. By combining your passion and expertise with market research and audience insights, you can carve out a unique space and attract a loyal following. Remember to constantly refine your content strategy, differentiate yourself from the competition, adapt to market trends, and engage with your audience consistently. Building a successful YouTube channel takes time, effort, and dedication, but by choosing your niche and target audience strategically, you'll be on your way to making millions from YouTube.

Keep the information provided in this chapter as a reference throughout your YouTube journey, as it will serve as a compass to navigate the vast opportunities and challenges that lie ahead.

Chapter 4

Exploring Different YouTuber Categories

YOUTUBE IS A DIVERSE platform with a wide range of content creators across various categories. In this chapter, we will explore some of the popular YouTuber categories and the unique aspects of each.

01-Vloggers and lifestyle YouTubers

In the vast digital landscape of YouTube, vloggers and lifestyle YouTubers have emerged as captivating content creators. They share their lives, passions, and adventures with the world, attracting enthusiastic fans who seek inspiration and valuable insights. These YouTubers come in various styles, inviting viewers into their personal journeys or providing expertise in specific areas of interest. Their candid storytelling creates a comforting space for viewers, while their knowledge and creativity make for an entertaining experience.

Beyond entertainment, these content creators inspire, motivate, and foster a sense of community. By watching their videos, viewers can explore new worlds, connect with like-minded individuals, and embrace their passions. Vloggers and lifestyle YouTubers offer a convenient avenue to discover, learn, and grow, making them a compelling choice for those seeking connection and personal growth.

02-Gaming YouTubers: Entertaining, Informative, and Inspiring

Gaming YouTubers have revolutionized the way people consume and engage with video game content. With their captivating videos and unique perspectives, they have garnered a massive following of fans who eagerly await their new uploads. These content creators are passionate about video games and cover a wide range of topics, from

gameplay walkthroughs and reviews to commentary and analysis. Their ability to immerse themselves in virtual worlds and share thrilling experiences with their audience is a major draw, appealing to both gamers and non-gamers alike. Whether they are playing the latest and most popular games or diving into the nostalgia of retro titles, gaming YouTubers provide entertainment, education, and inspiration.

Beyond entertainment, gaming YouTubers serve as valuable sources of knowledge and guidance for gamers. They offer in-depth tutorials, tips, and strategies to help viewers improve their skills and navigate the complexities of various games. By sharing their expertise and uncovering hidden secrets, they enhance the gaming experience for their audience.

Moreover, gaming YouTubers inspire and motivate their viewers by discussing their own gaming journeys, highlighting the positive aspects of gaming, and fostering a sense of community. Through their enthusiastic and inclusive approach, they encourage viewers to pursue their passions, explore new games, and connect with like-minded individuals. Overall, gaming YouTubers play a crucial role in shaping the gaming landscape, offering a diverse range of content that caters to the interests and needs of gamers worldwide.

03-Educational YouTubers

Educational YouTubers have revolutionized the way people learn and acquire knowledge online. These content creators are experts in their respective fields and use the power of video to deliver engaging and informative content to viewers worldwide. Whether you're a student, a professional, or simply curious about a specific subject, educational YouTubers offer a wealth of information in a dynamic and accessible format.

Through their videos, educational YouTubers break down complex topics into easily understandable chunks, employing visual aids, demonstrations, and clear explanations. They have mastered the art of making learning entertaining and enjoyable, capturing the attention of their audience and ensuring the information resonates. With their passion, expertise, and dedication to education, educational YouTubers have transformed the landscape of online learning, providing a valuable resource for individuals seeking to expand their knowledge and skills in a convenient and engaging way.

04-Comedy YouTubers

Comedy YouTubers have become a dominant force in the realm of online entertainment, captivating audiences with their comedic prowess and infectious humor. These content creators possess the unique ability to brighten your day and bring laughter into your life. Whether you're seeking an escape from reality or simply in need of a good chuckle, comedy YouTubers are there to deliver the comedic relief you crave. Beyond entertainment, comedy YouTubers have the power to uplift spirits and provide a much-needed break from the challenges of everyday life.

Laughter has a remarkable effect on our well-being, releasing endorphins and fostering a positive mindset. By immersing yourself in the comedic creations of these talented YouTubers, you allow yourself a moment of pure bliss and rejuvenation. Their channels become a sanctuary of humor, a place where you can momentarily set aside your worries and indulge in the healing power of laughter.

05-Food and cooking YouTubers

Food and cooking YouTubers have revolutionized the way we approach culinary arts. With their enticing videos, they offer a feast for the senses and a wealth of inspiration for aspiring home cooks and food enthusiasts. These creators bring a unique blend of recipes, cooking techniques, and food exploration, catering to a wide range of tastes and preferences.

From the comfort of our screens, we can embark on virtual food adventures, learning new recipes and discovering hidden culinary gems. These YouTubers serve as virtual mentors, guiding us through the art of

20

cooking, sharing their tips and tricks, and encouraging us to step outside our comfort zones.
With their infectious passion and mouth-watering creations, food and cooking YouTubers have transformed our kitchens into creative playgrounds and our meals into delightful experiences. So, join the foodie community, subscribe to your favorite channels, and let the culinary inspiration flow as you dive into the world of food and cooking on YouTube.

06-Fitness and wellness YouTubers

Fitness and wellness YouTubers have become a powerful force in inspiring individuals to prioritize their physical health, mental well-being, and personal growth. Through captivating videos, they offer workout routines, wholesome recipes, mindfulness techniques, and motivational content that empower viewers to embark on transformative journeys towards a healthier and happier life. Whether it's guiding viewers through exhilarating workout routines, providing guidance on mindfulness and self-care, or sharing personal stories of resilience and determination, these YouTubers create a supportive community that uplifts and inspires individuals worldwide.

What sets fitness and wellness YouTubers apart is their ability to bridge the gap between virtual and real-life experiences. While their content lives on screens, their impact extends far beyond pixels. Viewers not only witness physical transformations but also experience a shift in mindset. Motivated by the YouTubers' contagious energy, they incorporate healthier habits into their daily routines, find joy in physical activities, prioritize self-care, and cultivate resilience. The YouTube comments section becomes a space for individuals to share their successes, struggles, and newfound confidence, forming a vibrant support network.

By leveraging their platforms, fitness and wellness YouTubers are revolutionizing the way people approach their well-being, guiding them towards a path of self-improvement and lasting happiness.

21

07-Tech and Gadgets YouTubers

Tech and gadgets YouTubers have become an indispensable part of the technology landscape, captivating audiences with their expertise, enthusiasm, and unique perspectives. These content creators have carved out a niche in the vast realm of YouTube, serving as go-to sources for all things tech. Their in-depth reviews, unboxings, and tutorials provide valuable insights into the latest technological wonders, helping viewers make informed decisions about their tech purchases. Whether it's the newest smartphone, gaming console, or smart home device, these YouTubers dive deep into the features, performance, and user experience, offering a comprehensive understanding of the technology that shapes our lives.

What sets tech and gadgets YouTubers apart is their ability to masterfully combine entertainment and education. With their charismatic personalities and creative editing styles, they turn what could be mundane topics into captivating and enjoyable content. From witty commentary during gadget reviews to engaging challenges and experiments, these YouTubers bring a sense of excitement and intrigue to their videos.

Moreover, they go beyond simply showcasing the latest gadgets; they also empower viewers with the knowledge and skills to make the most of their technology. Through detailed tutorials and step-by-step guides, these virtual mentors demystify complex technologies and make them accessible to users of all skill levels. By doing so, they equip their audience with the necessary tools to navigate the digital world confidently and enhance their everyday lives

08-Travel and Adventure YouTubers

Travel and adventure YouTubers have revolutionized the way we explore and experience the world. With their captivating videos, they take us on thrilling journeys to mesmerizing destinations, immersing us in the beauty of different cultures, landscapes, and adventures. Through their

22

lens, we can trek through dense jungles, climb towering mountains, dive into pristine oceans, and wander through bustling cities, all from the comfort of our own screens. These intrepid content creators ignite our sense of wanderlust, inspire us to embrace new experiences, and empower us with valuable travel tips and insights, allowing us to embark on our own extraordinary adventures with confidence and enthusiasm.

Beyond showcasing stunning visuals, travel and adventure YouTubers foster a sense of community among like-minded travelers and culture enthusiasts. They celebrate the people, traditions, and customs that make each destination unique, promoting cross-cultural understanding and appreciation. Through their interactions with locals and their commitment to sustainable travel, they encourage responsible exploration and a deep respect for the natural and cultural heritage of the places we visit. By joining their virtual journeys, we become part of a global tribe of adventurers, united by our shared love for exploration, curiosity, and the boundless beauty our planet has to offer.

09-News and Current Events YouTubers

News and Current Events YouTubers have emerged as influential sources of information and analysis in today's digital age. With their unique approach to reporting, these content creators offer a fresh perspective on global events and bring important issues to the forefront. Through their videos, they provide a platform for in-depth discussions, insightful commentary, and diverse voices, ensuring that viewers are well-informed about the latest developments in politics, economics, social issues, and more.

News and Current Events YouTubers engage their audiences in thought-provoking conversations, challenging conventional narratives and sparking critical thinking. Their ability to break down complex topics in a digestible manner makes them invaluable sources of news for a generation that seeks alternative and independent media sources. Moreover, these YouTubers empower their viewers to be active participants in the news cycle. They encourage dialogue, foster engagement, and often involve their audience in shaping the content they produce.

23

By offering a more interactive and personalized approach to news, these creators bridge the gap between traditional media and the digital landscape, allowing individuals to stay informed, share their perspectives, and actively contribute to the discourse. With their dedication to journalistic integrity and a commitment to presenting balanced viewpoints, News and Current Events YouTubers have become influential voices that shape public opinion and contribute to the democratization of information in the digital era.

10-Podcasters and conversational YouTubers

Podcasters and conversational YouTubers have revolutionized the way we consume and engage with media content. With the rise of digital platforms, these individuals have found a unique way to connect with audiences and share their thoughts, ideas, and experiences through intimate conversations. Podcasters, in particular, have gained immense popularity due to their ability to create long-form discussions on a wide range of topics.

From true crime to self-improvement, comedy to politics, there is a podcast for everyone's interests. The conversational nature of these platforms allows hosts and guests to delve deep into subjects, providing a more in-depth analysis and fostering a sense of community among listeners. Through their engaging and often unscripted conversations, podcasters and conversational YouTubers offer a refreshing break from traditional media, allowing for a more personal and interactive experience.

Moreover, podcasters and conversational YouTubers have become influential voices in shaping public discourse and driving cultural conversations. With the freedom to express their opinions and invite diverse perspectives, these content creators have the ability to challenge mainstream narratives and provide alternative viewpoints. Listeners and viewers are drawn to the authenticity and relatability of these platforms, as they often feel like they are part of a conversation with friends rather than passively consuming information. This informal and conversational approach has also paved the way for niche communities and subcultures to thrive, as individuals with unique interests can find like-minded people and engage in discussions that were previously inaccessible. Overall,

24

podcasters and conversational YouTubers have transformed the media landscape, offering a refreshing and inclusive space for open dialogue, intellectual growth, and community building.

11-Motivational Speakers and Personal Development YouTubers

Motivational speakers and personal development YouTubers have become increasingly popular in recent years, as people seek guidance and inspiration to enhance their personal and professional lives. These individuals possess the unique ability to captivate audiences through their charismatic speaking styles and impactful messages. They delve into a wide range of topics, including goal setting, mindset shifts, overcoming challenges, and self-improvement techniques. Their aim is to empower individuals to unlock their full potential and live a fulfilling life.

Motivational speakers and personal development YouTubers offer a wealth of valuable information and practical strategies that can positively impact the lives of their viewers. By sharing personal stories, experiences, and lessons learned, they create a relatable and inspiring atmosphere that resonates with their audience. These individuals not only provide motivation but also offer actionable steps and tools to help individuals set meaningful goals, develop self-confidence, cultivate resilience, and navigate obstacles along their journey.

Through their online platforms, they have the power to reach and influence a global audience, making personal development accessible to anyone with an internet connection. Whether it's through thought-provoking speeches or engaging video content, motivational speakers and personal development YouTubers play a significant role in empowering individuals to unlock their true potential and create a life they love.

Chapter 5

Setting Up Your YouTube Channel

Welcome to Chapter 5 of "How to Make Millions from YouTube." Now that you have chosen your niche and identified your target audience, it's time to set up your YouTube channel. In this chapter, we will guide you through the process of creating a captivating channel that showcases your brand, engages your viewers, and sets the stage for your success. From channel branding to optimization techniques, we will cover all the essential elements you need to consider when setting up your YouTube channel.

Define Your Brand Identity

Before diving into the technical aspects of setting up your channel, it's crucial to establish a clear brand identity. Your brand identity encompasses the essence of your channel, including its values, mission, and personality. Define your brand's unique selling points, tone of voice, and visual style. Think about the feelings you want to arouse in your viewers and how you want them to perceive your channel. This cohesive brand identity will help you create consistent and compelling content that resonates with your viewers.

Choose an Engaging Channel Name

Your channel name is the first impression viewers have of your brand, so it's important to choose a name that is memorable, descriptive, and aligned with your niche. Ideally, your channel name should reflect your content and make it easy for viewers to understand what your channel is about. Avoid generic names and instead opt for something catchy and unique that sets you apart from the competition. Perform a thorough search to ensure that the chosen name is available and not trademarked by others.

Create a Captivating Channel Art

Channel art, including the banner and profile picture, is the visual representation of your brand on YouTube. It's essential to create captivating and professional-looking channel art that grabs the attention of viewers and communicates your brand identity. Design a banner that incorporates your channel name, showcases your niche, and represents your style. Use high-resolution images, relevant graphics, and eye-catching colors. Ensure that the channel art is optimized for different devices to maintain its visual appeal across desktop and mobile platforms.

Craft a Compelling Channel Trailer

A channel trailer is a brief video that introduces new viewers to your channel and gives them a taste of your content. It's an opportunity to showcase your personality, highlight your best content, and communicate the value viewers can expect from your channel. Keep your channel trailer concise, engaging, and well-edited. Use it as a tool to hook potential subscribers and encourage them to explore more of your content. Don't forget to include a strong call-to-action, such as subscribing or watching a popular video.

Optimize Your Channel Description and About Section

Your channel description and about section play a vital role in telling viewers what your channel is all about and enticing them to subscribe. Craft a compelling and concise channel description that clearly explains your niche, unique value proposition, and the benefits viewers can gain from subscribing to your channel. Use relevant keywords to optimize your description for search engines. In the about section, provide more details about yourself, your background, and any relevant achievements or credentials that establish your authority in your niche.

Select the Right Channel Categories and Tags

Categorizing your channel and using appropriate tags is crucial for YouTube's search algorithm and helps viewers discover your content. Choose the most relevant category for your channel to ensure it appears in the right search results and recommendations. Additionally, utilize relevant tags when uploading videos to provide context and improve discoverability. Research popular tags within your niche, use a mix of broad and specific tags, and monitor trends to stay current and optimize your channel's visibility.

Customize Your Thumbnails and Video End Screens

Thumbnails and end screens are powerful tools for attracting viewers and encouraging engagement. Create eye-catching thumbnails that accurately represent your video's content and evoke curiosity. Use vibrant colors, clear images, and compelling text overlays to make your thumbnails stand out in search results and recommendations. Additionally, design visually appealing and informative end screens that encourage viewers to take the desired actions, such as subscribing, watching another video, or visiting your website. Customize your end screens to provide a seamless and engaging viewing experience while promoting your channel's growth.

Set Up Playlists and Sections

Organizing your content through playlists and sections helps viewers navigate your channel easily and find the videos that interest them. Create thematic playlists that group together related videos, making it convenient for viewers to binge-watch content on specific topics. Consider creating an introductory playlist for new subscribers and a "Best of" playlist that features your most popular or highest-quality videos. Use sections to highlight featured content, recent uploads, or collaborations with other creators. By organizing your channel effectively, you enhance the user experience and increase the likelihood of viewers spending more time on your channel.

Establish a Consistent Upload Schedule

Consistency is key when it comes to building an engaged audience on YouTube. Establishing a regular upload schedule helps your viewers anticipate new content and builds trust and loyalty. Determine how frequently you can create high-quality videos without compromising their value. Whether it's once a week, twice a month, or any other schedule that suits your niche and production capabilities, communicate your upload schedule to your viewers and stick to it. Consistency in content delivery is essential for retaining and growing your subscriber base.

Utilize YouTube Analytics for Insights

YouTube Analytics provides valuable data and insights about your channel's performance, audience demographics, and viewer behavior. Regularly review your analytics to gain a deeper understanding of what content resonates with your audience, which videos attract the most views and engagement, and where your viewers are coming from. Use these insights to refine your content strategy, identify trends, and make informed decisions that drive channel growth and revenue. Continuously monitor your analytics to adapt and optimize your channel based on viewer preferences and trends.

Setting up your YouTube channel is a crucial step towards building a successful and lucrative presence on the platform. By carefully crafting your brand identity, creating captivating channel art, optimizing your descriptions and tags, and organizing your content effectively, you can attract and engage your target audience. Remember to prioritize consistency in uploading content and utilize

YouTube Analytics to gain insights and make data-driven decisions. A well-structured and optimized channel lays the foundation for success and positions you for long-term growth and profitability on YouTube.

In the next chapter, we will dive into the art of creating compelling and high-quality content that captivates your audience and keeps them coming back for more. Stay tuned and get ready to unlock the secrets of producing videos that stand out in the vast YouTube landscape.

Chapter 6

Creating High-Quality Content

WELCOME TO CHAPTER 6 of "How to Make Millions from YouTube." In this chapter, we will explore the essential strategies and techniques for creating high-quality content that will captivate your audience, drive engagement, and ultimately help you achieve success on YouTube. Creating compelling and valuable content is the foundation of a thriving YouTube channel, and in this chapter, we will delve into the key elements that will set your videos apart from the competition.

Before you start creating content, it's crucial to have a clear understanding of your target audience. Who are they? What are their interests, needs, and desires? Understanding your audience will help you develop videos that appeal to them and cater your content to their interests.

Researching popular trends and topics within your niche can help you identify what your target audience is currently interested in.

Use tools like Google Trends, YouTube Analytics, and social media platforms to gain insights into popular topics, keywords, and search trends. By staying up to date with what's trending, you can create content that is relevant and appealing to your audience.

Unique Value Proposition

To stand out in the vast sea of YouTube content, you need a unique value proposition. What makes your videos different from others in your niche? How will viewers benefit from watching your content? Defining your unique value proposition will give you a competitive edge and attract an audience that resonates with your style and message.

Think about your strengths, expertise, and passion. Consider how you can leverage your unique qualities to offer something valuable to your viewers. Whether it's providing informative tutorials, entertaining storytelling, or inspiring vlogs, focus on delivering content that sets you apart and provides a distinct value proposition.

Compelling Titles and Thumbnails

Creating eye-catching titles and thumbnails is crucial for grabbing the attention of potential viewers. Your video's title and thumbnail are the first things people see when scrolling through YouTube, and they play a significant role in whether someone clicks on your video or not.

Craft compelling and concise titles that accurately represent the content of your video while piquing curiosity. Incorporate keywords relevant to your topic to increase discoverability in search results. Additionally, experiment with different thumbnail designs that are visually appealing, well-composed, and convey the essence of your video. High-quality and enticing thumbnails will entice viewers to click and watch your content.

Engaging Content Structure

When it comes to creating high-quality content, structure and organization are essential. Plan your videos in advance and outline the key points you want to cover. A well-structured video will help you communicate your message clearly, keep your audience engaged, and avoid rambling or going off-topic.

Begin each video with a strong hook that captures viewers' attention within the first few seconds. Clearly introduce the topic and outline what viewers can expect from the video. Break down your content into sections or segments to make it easier to follow. Use visual aids, such as on-screen graphics, text overlays, or relevant B-roll footage, to enhance the visual appeal and reinforce your message.

Compelling Storytelling and Personality

One of the most powerful ways to connect with your audience is through compelling storytelling and showcasing your unique personality. People are drawn to authenticity and relatability, so don't be afraid to inject your own experiences, anecdotes, or humor into your videos. This personal touch will help you build a loyal community of viewers who feel a genuine connection with you.

Craft your videos in a way that takes your viewers on a journey. Develop a narrative arc that engages emotions, sparks curiosity, and keeps viewers hooked until the end. Use visuals, music, and editing techniques to enhance the storytelling experience and create a compelling narrative flow.

Delivering Value and Solving Problems

One of the most effective ways to create high-quality content is by providing value and solving problems for your viewers. Think about the needs and challenges of your target audience and create content that addresses those issues. Whether it's sharing expert advice, offering practical tips and tutorials, or providing in-depth analyses, your content should aim to help your viewers overcome obstacles and achieve their goals.

Research common questions and problems within your niche and develop content that offers solutions. Conduct interviews with experts, share case studies, or provide step-by-step guides that empower your viewers to take action. Delivering high-quality content on a regular basis will help you establish your authority in your industry and draw in a committed audience.

Sound and image quality

Creating high-quality content goes beyond just the information you provide. The visual and audio aspects of your videos play a significant role in how your content is perceived. Invest in good quality equipment, such as cameras, microphones, and lighting, to ensure clear visuals and crisp audio. Poor video and audio quality can distract viewers and diminish the overall impact of your content.

Pay attention to the composition of your shots, framing your subject well, and ensuring good lighting conditions. Use editing software to enhance the visual appeal of your videos, such as color correction, adding transitions, and incorporating engaging visual effects when appropriate. Additionally, make sure your audio is clear and free from background noise. Invest in a good microphone and edit the audio to optimize volume levels and reduce any unwanted noise.

Engagement and Interaction

Creating high-quality content goes hand in hand with fostering engagement and interaction with your viewers. Encourage your audience to participate by asking questions, requesting feedback, and inviting them to share their thoughts and experiences in the comments section. Respond to comments, engage in discussions, and make an effort to build a community around your content.

Consider incorporating interactive elements within your videos, such as polls, quizzes, or challenges that viewers can participate in. This not only increases engagement but also gives your audience a sense of involvement and ownership in your content. When viewers feel heard and valued, they are more likely to become loyal fans and advocates for your channel.

Consistency and Optimization

Consistency is key when it comes to creating high-quality content on YouTube. Set a regular upload schedule and stick to it. Consistency builds trust with your audience and keeps them coming back for more. Plan and batch-produce your content in advance to ensure a consistent flow of videos.

Optimize your videos for search engines by incorporating relevant keywords in your titles, descriptions, and tags. Use YouTube's search suggestions and keyword research tools to identify popular keywords in your niche. Additionally, make sure to include a compelling video description that provides a concise summary of your content and encourages viewers to watch.

Promotion and Collaboration

Creating high-quality content is only part of the equation. Promoting your videos and collaborating with other creators can significantly expand your reach and attract new viewers to your channel. Share your videos on social media platforms, engage with relevant online communities, and consider reaching out to influencers or other YouTube creators for potential collaborations.

Collaborations not only expose your content to a new audience but also provide an opportunity to learn from other creators and tap into their expertise. Look for creators whose content aligns with yours or who have a complementary audience. Collaborative videos can take various forms, such as interviews, guest appearances, or joint projects. By leveraging the power of collaboration, you can accelerate the growth of your YouTube channel.

Creating high-quality content is the cornerstone of success on YouTube. By understanding your target audience, delivering value, and showcasing your unique personality, you can create videos that captivate viewers and build a loyal community. Remember to pay attention to visual and audio quality, foster engagement and interaction, and remain consistent in your content creation.

Chapter 7

Building Your Subscriber Base

Welcome to Chapter 7 of "How to Make Millions from YouTube." In this chapter, we will explore the strategies and techniques for building a strong and engaged subscriber base on YouTube. Your subscribers are the lifeblood of your channel, and by growing your subscriber count, you increase your reach, influence, and ultimately your potential for earning millions from YouTube. So, let's dive into the essential steps for building your subscriber base.

The foundation of attracting and retaining subscribers lies in consistently delivering high-quality content. Remember, quality trumps quantity. Focus on creating videos that are informative, entertaining, or valuable to your target audience. Strive to provide content that is unique, well-researched, and meets the needs and interests of your viewers.

Maintain a regular upload schedule that your subscribers can rely on. Consistency builds trust and keeps your audience engaged.

However, don't sacrifice quality for the sake of meeting deadlines. It's better to produce exceptional content less frequently than to publish subpar videos on a daily basis.

Optimize Video Titles, Descriptions, and Tags

Optimizing your videos for search engines is crucial for attracting new subscribers. Utilize relevant keywords in your video titles, descriptions, and tags to increase discoverability. Conduct keyword research using tools like Google Trends, YouTube Analytics, or third-party software to identify popular search terms in your niche.

Craft compelling and concise video titles that accurately represent your content while piquing curiosity. Your video descriptions should provide a concise summary of the video, incorporating relevant keywords naturally. Additionally, use tags strategically to categorize and index your videos effectively.

Engaging Thumbnails and Titles

Thumbnails and titles are the gateways to your videos. They play a significant role in attracting viewers' attention and enticing them to click and watch. Create visually appealing thumbnails that stand out from the competition. Use bold, eye-catching imagery, clear text, and contrasting colors to make your thumbnails pop.

Align your thumbnail design with the content of your video, ensuring it accurately represents the essence of your video. A strong and enticing thumbnail paired with a compelling title increases the click-through rate and helps build your subscriber base.

Call-to-Action and Subscription Reminders

Never underestimate the power of a well-placed call-to-action (CTA). Encourage viewers to subscribe to your channel by including subscription reminders throughout your videos. Remind them to click the subscribe button, hit the notification bell, and join your community of subscribers.

Place CTAs strategically, such as at the beginning or end of your videos, and consider using annotations or end screens to direct viewers to subscribe. Additionally, include verbal reminders during your videos, expressing gratitude for their support and inviting them to become part of your channel's community.

Collaborations and Shoutouts

Collaborating with other YouTube creators can significantly boost your subscriber count. Seek out creators in your niche or those with a similar target audience and propose collaborations. Collaborative videos can take various forms, such as interviews, challenges, or joint projects.

When collaborating, you gain exposure to the audience of the creator you're partnering with. This cross-promotion introduces your channel to new viewers who may be interested in your content, thereby increasing your subscriber base. Don't forget to return the favor by promoting your collaborators on your own channel.

Engage with Your Audience

Building a strong subscriber base involves fostering a sense of community and engagement. Respond to comments on your videos and engage in discussions with your viewers. Show appreciation for their support and take the time to address their questions, feedback, and suggestions.

Consider creating videos based on viewer requests or conducting Q&A sessions to involve your audience directly. By actively engaging with your subscribers, you demonstrate that you value their input and create a connection that encourages them to become loyal subscribers.

Utilize YouTube Features

YouTube offers various features that can help you engage with your audience and attract new subscribers. Take advantage of these features to maximize your channel's growth potential.

a. Community Tab: Utilize the Community tab to share updates, behind-the-scenes content, polls, and exclusive content with your subscribers. This feature allows for direct interaction and keeps your audience engaged.

b. YouTube Live: Go live on YouTube to connect with your audience in real-time. Host live Q&A sessions, tutorials, or interactive events that encourage viewers to subscribe and participate actively.

c. YouTube Premiere: Use YouTube Premiere to create anticipation and buzz around your upcoming videos. This feature allows you to schedule a video release and engage with your subscribers in a live chat as the video premieres.

d. Cards and End Screens: Incorporate interactive elements like cards and end screens in your videos. Use these features to promote other relevant videos, playlists, or encourage viewers to subscribe to your channel.

Cross-Promotion on Social Media

Expand your reach beyond YouTube by leveraging the power of social media platforms. Promote your videos, channel, and upcoming content on platforms like Instagram, Twitter, Facebook, or TikTok. Utilize their unique features, such as hashtags, stories, or reels, to generate interest and direct traffic to your YouTube channel.

Engage with your social media followers by sharing behind-the-scenes content, teasers, or snippets of your videos. Encourage them to subscribe to your channel to access full content and be part of your YouTube community.

Encourage Subscribers to Share and Spread the Word

Word-of-mouth is a powerful tool for attracting new subscribers. Encourage your existing subscribers to share your videos with their friends, family, or on their social media platforms. Include a CTA in your videos, requesting viewers to share your content if they found it valuable or entertaining.

You can also incentivize sharing by running contests or giveaways exclusively for your subscribers. By rewarding their efforts and engagement, you create a sense of excitement and encourage them to spread the word about your channel.

Monitor Analytics and Learn from Insights

Regularly monitor your YouTube Analytics to gain insights into your channel's performance. Pay attention to metrics like watch time, audience retention, subscriber growth, and engagement. Analyzing this data will help you understand what type of content resonates with your audience and identify areas for improvement.

Take note of your most successful videos in terms of subscriber growth and engagement. Analyze the common elements that contributed to their success and replicate those strategies in future videos. Learn from your analytics to refine your content strategy and continue building your subscriber base.

Building a strong and engaged subscriber base is crucial for achieving success on YouTube. By consistently providing high-quality content, optimizing your videos, engaging with your audience, and leveraging promotional strategies, you can steadily grow your subscriber count. Remember, building a subscriber base takes time and effort, so stay committed, adapt to the changing landscape, and continue refining your content to attract and retain loyal subscribers. With dedication and the right strategies, you can position yourself for long-term success and the potential to make millions from YouTube.

Chapter 8

Optimizing Video Titles, Descriptions, and Tags

WELCOME TO CHAPTER 8 of "How to Make Millions from YouTube." In this chapter, we will dive deep into the world of optimizing video titles, descriptions, and tags. These elements play a crucial role in helping your videos rank higher in search results, attract more viewers, and ultimately increase your chances of making millions on YouTube. So, let's get started and learn the secrets to creating compelling titles, engaging descriptions, and effective tags for your videos.

Crafting Attention-Grabbing Video Titles

Your video title is the first thing potential viewers see when they come across your content. It's your chance to make a strong impression and entice them to click and watch your video. Here are some tips to create attention-grabbing video titles:

Be Clear and Concise: Keep your title concise and to the point. Clearly communicate what your video is about, using keywords that are relevant to your content.

Use Keywords Strategically: Incorporate relevant keywords into your titles to improve search visibility. Research popular keywords and phrases using tools like Google Keyword Planner or YouTube's autocomplete feature.

Be Unique and Creative: Stand out from the competition by crafting unique and creative titles. Think of ways to intrigue viewers and make them curious about your video's content.

Include Numbers and Power Words: Incorporate numbers or power words in your titles to capture attention. For example, "10 Essential Tips," "The Ultimate Guide," or "Secrets Revealed."

Crafting Engaging Video Descriptions

The video description is an opportunity to provide more information about your video, engage viewers, and improve your search rankings. Here's how you can create engaging video descriptions:

Start with a Hook: Begin your description with a compelling hook that grabs the reader's attention. Pose a question, share an interesting fact, or create a sense of curiosity to encourage viewers to continue reading.

Summarize the Video: Provide a brief summary of what viewers can expect from your video. Highlight the main points or key takeaways to give them a clear idea of what they will learn or experience.

Include Relevant Links: If you have a website, blog, or social media profiles, include links in your description. This allows viewers to explore more of your content and increases traffic to your other platforms.

Utilize Keywords: Incorporate relevant keywords naturally throughout your description. This can help search engines understand the context of your video and improve its visibility in search results.

Add Timestamps: If your video covers different topics or sections, consider adding timestamps in the description. This allows viewers to navigate easily through the content and find specific sections they're interested in.

Optimizing Video Tags

Video tags are labels that help YouTube's algorithm understand the content of your video. They play a crucial role in search ranking and can help your video appear in the "related videos" section. The following tips will help you properly optimise your video tags:

Use a Variety of Tags: Include a mix of broad and specific tags. Broad tags describe the overall topic of your video, while specific tags highlight niche keywords related to your content.

Research Competitors: Look at the tags used by popular YouTubers or channels in your niche. This can provide insights into relevant tags and help you discover new ideas for your own videos.

Long-Tail Keywords: Incorporate long-tail keywords in your tags. These are more specific and less competitive, increasing the chances of your video ranking higher in search results.

Relevance is Key: Ensure that your tags accurately reflect the content of your video. Using misleading or irrelevant tags may lead to a negative user experience and can harm your channel's reputation.

Utilize YouTube's Autocomplete: Take advantage of YouTube's autocomplete feature when adding tags. This feature suggests popular search queries related to your video's topic, giving you valuable keyword ideas.

Tag Optimization Tools: Consider using tag optimization tools such as TubeBuddy or VidIQ. These tools provide insights into keyword popularity, competition, and can help you choose the most effective tags for your videos.

Experiment and Analyze: Don't be afraid to experiment with different tags and monitor their performance. Analyze your video's analytics to see which tags are driving the most traffic and engagement, and refine your tag strategy accordingly.

Best Practices for Optimizing Titles, Descriptions, and Tags

Now that we've covered the specific elements of optimizing video titles, descriptions, and tags, let's go over some best practices to keep in mind:

Consistency: Maintain consistency across your titles, descriptions, and tags. This helps build a strong brand identity and makes it easier for viewers to recognize your content.

Avoid Clickbait: While it's important to create attention-grabbing titles, it's equally important to avoid misleading or clickbait titles. Misleading viewers will harm your reputation and can result in negative feedback or decreased engagement.

Think Like a Viewer: Put yourself in the shoes of your target audience. What would they search for? What would catch their attention? Tailor your titles, descriptions, and tags to appeal to their interests and needs.

Monitor Trends: Stay updated with the latest trends and topics in your niche. Incorporate relevant keywords and phrases into your titles, descriptions, and tags to capitalize on the current buzz and increase your video's visibility.

Regularly Update and Optimize: Optimization is an ongoing process. Regularly review and update your video titles, descriptions, and tags based on feedback, analytics, and changing trends. This ensures that your content remains relevant and continues to attract new viewers.

Optimizing video titles, descriptions, and tags is a crucial step in increasing your YouTube channel's visibility and attracting a larger audience. By crafting attention-grabbing titles, engaging descriptions, and utilizing effective tags, you can improve your search rankings, increase click-through rates, and ultimately make millions from YouTube.

Remember to be clear, concise, and creative with your titles. Craft engaging descriptions that provide valuable information and utilize relevant keywords. Lastly, optimize your tags using a mix of broad and specific terms, while staying true to the content of your video.

By following these optimization strategies and best practices, you'll be well on your way to maximizing your YouTube success and reaching millions of viewers with your compelling content. Happy optimizing!

Chapter 9

Utilizing Thumbnails and Video Graphics

In the fast-paced world of YouTube, capturing the attention of viewers is crucial for your success. With millions of videos being uploaded every day, standing out from the crowd can be challenging. That's where thumbnails and video graphics come into play. They are powerful tools that can make a significant impact on your channel's growth and engagement. In this chapter, we will explore the art of creating compelling thumbnails and video graphics that will grab the attention of your audience and increase your chances of making millions from YouTube.

The Power of Thumbnails:

When a user is scrolling through videos on YouTube, thumbnails are the first thing they see. They act as a visual representation of your content and play a vital role in attracting viewers to click on your video. A well-designed thumbnail can make all the difference between someone scrolling past your video or deciding to watch it.

Clear and Engaging Visuals:

When creating a thumbnail, aim for clarity and engagement. Use high-resolution images that are relevant to your video's content. Avoid cluttered and confusing visuals that may deter viewers from clicking. The image should be eye-catching and easily understandable, even at a small size.

Highlight Your Video's Value:

A great thumbnail not only grabs attention but also communicates the value of your video. Include text or graphics that convey what the viewer can expect from watching your content. Whether it's a tutorial, a funny moment, or a captivating story, make sure your thumbnail reflects the essence of your video.

Choose Vibrant Colors:

Colors can have a significant impact on viewers' perception and emotions. Experiment with vibrant and contrasting colors to make your thumbnail stand out. However, be cautious not to overdo it, as excessive use of colors can make your thumbnail look chaotic and unprofessional.

Consistency and Branding:

Establishing a consistent visual style across your thumbnails helps viewers recognize your content instantly. Incorporate your brand colors, logo, or a recognizable element that ties all your videos together. Consistency builds trust and credibility, making viewers more likely to click on your videos.

Creating Engaging Video Graphics:

While thumbnails are essential for attracting viewers, video graphics play a crucial role in keeping them engaged throughout the video. Graphics can enhance the viewing experience, provide additional information, and reinforce your brand identity.

Lower Thirds and Text Overlays:

Lower thirds are graphical elements that display text at the bottom of the screen, often used to introduce speakers, provide context, or highlight key points. Use lower thirds sparingly and ensure that the text is legible and does not obstruct important visuals. Consider using text overlays to emphasize important information or create visual interest within your videos.

Intro and Outro Graphics:

An engaging intro and outro can leave a lasting impression on your viewers. Create a visually appealing intro that showcases your channel's branding and sets the tone for your content. Similarly, an outro can include call-to-action buttons, links to related videos, or subscribe prompts to encourage viewers to further engage with your channel.

Visual Demonstrations and Illustrations:

If your content involves complex concepts or instructions, consider using graphics to simplify and enhance understanding. Visual demonstrations, arrows, icons, and illustrations can help guide viewers and make your videos more engaging. Make sure the graphics are clear, relevant, and not overwhelming.

Transitions and Animations:

Your films can become more polished and appealing by using smooth transitions and subtle animations. Utilize transition effects to create a seamless flow between scenes or segments. However, avoid using excessive or distracting animations that may overshadow your content.

The first half of the struggle is making eye-catching thumbnails and video visuals. To make the most of these elements, you need to optimize them for maximum visibility and engagement.

A/B Testing:

Performing A/B testing with your thumbnails can help you understand which designs resonate better with your audience. Create multiple variations of thumbnails for the same video and test them against each other to see which one generates more clicks and views. Analyze the data and make informed decisions on which designs to use in the future.

Keyword Research:

Just like optimizing your video titles and descriptions, incorporating relevant keywords in your thumbnails and video graphics can improve their discoverability. Conduct keyword research to identify popular search terms related to your content. Use these keywords strategically in the text overlays or image descriptions to attract viewers who are searching for specific topics.

Thumbnail Consistency:

Maintain consistency in your thumbnail style across your channel. This consistency helps build brand recognition and establishes a visual identity for your content. When viewers recognize your thumbnail style, they are more likely to associate it with quality and click on your videos consistently.

Mobile-Friendly Design:

With the majority of YouTube viewers accessing content on mobile devices, it's crucial to ensure your thumbnails and video graphics are optimized for mobile viewing. Keep the text and visuals clear and legible even at smaller sizes. Test how your thumbnails appear on mobile devices to ensure they are appealing and effective.

Monitor Analytics:

Regularly monitor your analytics to gain insights into how your thumbnails and video graphics are performing. Look at metrics such as click-through rates, views, and watch time to understand which designs are resonating with your audience. Use this data to iterate and improve your thumbnail and graphics strategy over time.

Thumbnails and video graphics are powerful tools that can significantly impact your success on YouTube. By creating compelling, visually appealing, and relevant thumbnails, you can capture viewers' attention and entice them to click on your videos. Similarly, using engaging video graphics enhances the viewing experience and reinforces your brand identity.

By optimizing these elements and continuously monitoring their performance, you can increase your chances of making millions from YouTube. Remember to be creative, experiment, and adapt your strategies based on audience feedback and trends. With thoughtful and captivating thumbnails and video graphics, you can make your mark in the competitive world of YouTube and build a thriving channel.

Part II
Monetizing Your YouTube Channel

Chapter 10

Joining the YouTube Partner Program

Congratulations! You've reached an exciting milestone on your journey to YouTube stardom. In this chapter, we will delve into the world of the YouTube Partner Program, a gateway to monetizing your content and potentially making millions from YouTube. Buckle up, because we're about to explore the steps you need to take to join this exclusive program.

Understanding the YouTube Partner Program

The YouTube Partner Program (YPP) is a system designed to reward content creators for their hard work and dedication. By joining the program, you gain access to various monetization features that can help you generate revenue from your YouTube channel. This includes earning money from advertisements, channel memberships, Super Chat, and YouTube Premium revenue.

Eligibility Requirements

Before you can dive into the YouTube Partner Program, you need to ensure that you meet the eligibility criteria. These requirements are in place to maintain a certain level of quality and protect the integrity of the platform. Here are the key qualifications you need to fulfill:

a. Follow YouTube's monetization policies: Your channel must adhere to YouTube's guidelines and policies regarding copyright, community standards, and advertiser-friendly content.

b. Meet the minimum requirements: You need to have at least 1,000 subscribers on your YouTube channel and a minimum of 4,000 watch hours in the past 12 months.

c. Have an AdSense account: The YouTube Partner Program is connected to Google AdSense, a platform that handles the financial side of monetization. Make sure you have an AdSense account linked to your YouTube channel.

Building Your Subscriber Base and Watch Hours

To meet the eligibility criteria, you may need to put in some additional effort to grow your subscriber base and watch hours. Here are some strategies to help you reach those goals:

a. Create compelling content: Focus on producing high-quality videos that resonate with your target audience. Invest time in planning, scripting, filming, and editing to ensure your videos stand out from the crowd.

b. Optimize your video titles, descriptions, and tags: Use relevant keywords to help YouTube's algorithm understand the content of your videos and improve their visibility in search results.

c. Promote your channel: Leverage social media platforms, collaborate with other creators, and engage with your viewers to expand your reach and attract new subscribers.

d. Consistency is key: Regularly upload new content to keep your audience engaged and encourage them to come back for more.

Applying to the YouTube Partner Program

Once you've met the eligibility requirements, it's time to apply for the YouTube Partner Program. Follow these steps to initiate the application process:

a. Sign in to your YouTube account and go to YouTube Studio.

b. In the left-hand menu, click on "Monetization" and then select "Enable."

c. Follow the on-screen instructions to review and accept the terms of the YouTube Partner Program.

d. Connect your YouTube channel to an AdSense account if you haven't done so already.

e. Set up monetization preferences, such as ad formats and placements.

f. Wait for YouTube to review your application. This process can take several weeks, so be patient.

Maintaining Your Partnership

Once you're accepted into the YouTube Partner Program, you have unlocked the potential to earn significant revenue. However, it's crucial to maintain the quality and compliance that got you there in the first place. Here are some tips to ensure your continued success:

a. Adhere to YouTube's policies: Stay updated with YouTube's guidelines and policies to avoid any content violations or community strikes that could jeopardize your partnership.

b. Engage with your audience: Respond to comments, create a sense of community, and make your viewers feel valued. Building a loyal fan base can lead to increased viewership and engagement, ultimately boosting your revenue potential.

c. Diversify your revenue streams: While ad revenue is a significant part of monetization, explore other avenues such as sponsored content, merchandise sales, brand partnerships, and crowdfunding to maximize your earnings.

d. Analyze your analytics: Utilize YouTube Analytics to gain insights into your audience demographics, watch time, and video performance. This data will help you make informed decisions about content creation and optimization strategies.

e. Stay consistent and upload regularly: Maintaining a consistent uploading schedule is essential for retaining and growing your subscriber base. Regular uploads keep your channel active and increase your chances of appearing in viewers' recommendations.

f. Continue to improve your content: Always strive to enhance the quality of your videos. Invest in better equipment, improve your editing skills, and listen to feedback from your audience to refine your content.

g. Network and collaborate with other creators: Building relationships within the YouTube community can open doors to collaborations, cross-promotion, and exposure to new audiences. Collaborating with established creators can provide a significant boost to your channel's growth.

Maximizing Monetization Opportunities

Now that you're a part of the YouTube Partner Program, it's time to maximize your monetization opportunities. Here are some strategies to help you make the most of your partnership:

a. Optimize your ad placements: Experiment with different ad formats and placements to find the right balance between viewer experience and revenue generation. Consider mid-roll ads, end screens, and strategically placed ad breaks.

b. Explore channel memberships and Super Chat: Channel memberships allow your most dedicated fans to pay a monthly fee in exchange for exclusive perks. Super Chat enables viewers to pay to have their messages highlighted during live chats. Encourage your audience to participate in these features to boost your earnings.

c. Leverage YouTube Premium revenue: YouTube Premium subscribers contribute to a separate revenue pool that is distributed among creators based on their viewership. Encourage your audience to subscribe to YouTube Premium to increase your revenue potential.

d. Utilize affiliate marketing: Partner with relevant brands and include affiliate links in your video descriptions. When viewers make purchases through your links, you earn a commission. Ensure that the products or services you promote align with your channel's content and audience interests.

e. Explore brand partnerships: As your channel grows, you may attract the attention of brands interested in collaborating with you. Sponsored content and brand partnerships can provide substantial financial opportunities. However, be selective and ensure the partnerships align with your values and resonate with your audience.

Never Stop Learning and Evolving

The world of YouTube is ever-evolving, and to stay ahead, you must continuously learn and adapt. Keep up with the latest trends, algorithm changes, and audience preferences. Experiment with new video formats, engage with your viewers, and embrace innovation. Remember, the most successful creators are those who are open to change and willing to evolve their content.

Joining the YouTube Partner Program is an exciting step toward monetizing your content and potentially making millions from YouTube. By meeting the eligibility requirements, maintaining high-quality content, and exploring various monetization avenues, you can turn your passion into a lucrative career. Remember, success on YouTube requires perseverance, dedication, and a willingness to adapt. Embrace the journey, learn from your experiences, and keep creating amazing content. The sky's the limit!

Chapter 11

Understanding Ad Revenue and CPM

In this chapter, we will delve into the world of ad revenue and CPM, two crucial factors that can significantly impact your earnings as a YouTube content creator. Understanding how these components work and how to optimize them can help you unlock the true potential of your YouTube channel and pave the way to financial success. So, let's dive right in and explore the intricacies of ad revenue and CPM.

Ad Revenue: The Driving Force Behind Your Earnings

Ad revenue forms the backbone of monetization for most YouTube creators. It is the income generated by displaying ads on your videos, and it is directly influenced by the number of ads shown and the amount advertisers are willing to pay for those ads. The more ads you have on your videos and the higher the prices advertisers are willing to pay, the greater your potential earnings.

Understanding CPM: Cost per Mille

CPM, which stands for "Cost per Mille" (mille means a thousand in Latin), is a critical metric that measures the price an advertiser pays for every thousand ad impressions. It represents the revenue generated for content creators for every thousand ad views on their videos. CPM rates can vary widely, depending on factors such as the audience demographics, the niche of your content, and the ad format being used.

Factors Affecting CPM Rates

Audience Demographics: Advertisers value certain demographics more than others. For example, if your content attracts a highly sought-after demographic, such as young adults with disposable income, advertisers may be willing to pay a premium to target that audience. On the other hand, if your audience consists primarily of younger viewers or those without much purchasing power, CPM rates may be lower.

Content Niche: The topic and niche of your videos also play a role in determining CPM rates. Advertisers may be willing to pay more to advertise on content that aligns with their products or services. For instance, if your channel focuses on technology reviews and you have a tech-savvy audience, tech companies may be more inclined to advertise on your videos, leading to higher CPM rates.

Ad Format and Placement: The format and placement of ads on your videos can impact CPM rates as well. Pre-roll ads that appear before your video generally have higher CPM rates compared to mid-roll or overlay ads. Advertisers often prefer pre-roll ads because they have a higher chance of capturing viewers' attention. However, it is important to strike a balance between monetization and user experience, as too many intrusive ads can negatively affect your audience's viewing experience and overall engagement.

Optimizing Ad Revenue and CPM

Build a Targeted Audience: Focus on creating content that caters to a specific niche and target audience. By attracting a dedicated following, you increase your chances of attracting advertisers who are interested in reaching that specific audience.

Increase audience engagement: Promote liking, commenting, and sharing of your videos among your audience. Higher engagement signals to advertisers that your audience is actively involved, making your channel more attractive for ad placements and potentially increasing CPM rates.

Improve Video Quality: Invest in high-quality equipment, editing software, and production value. High-quality videos tend to attract more viewers and keep them engaged for longer periods, increasing the likelihood of ad impressions and higher CPM rates.

Experiment with Ad Formats: Test different ad formats to find the right balance between monetization and user experience. Consider using a mix of pre-roll, mid-roll, and overlay ads to optimize your revenue while keeping your viewers engaged.

Collaborate with Brands: Seek out brand partnerships and collaborations that align with your content. Partnering with relevant brands not only provides an additional revenue stream but also demonstrates to advertisers that your channel is a valuable platform for reaching their target audience. These partnerships can lead to sponsored videos or integrations, which often command higher CPM rates compared to standard ads.

Optimize Ad Placement: Experiment with the placement of ads within your videos. While pre-roll ads are typically the most lucrative, strategically placing mid-roll ads at natural breaks in your content can also generate significant revenue without disrupting the viewing experience too much. Additionally, utilizing overlay ads sparingly but effectively can provide supplementary income.

Utilize YouTube's Monetization Features: YouTube offers various features to help maximize your ad revenue. For instance, you can enable channel memberships, which allow your most dedicated fans to support you through monthly payments in exchange for exclusive perks. You can also utilize Super Chat and Super Stickers during live streams to encourage viewer donations. Leveraging these features can supplement your ad revenue and increase overall earnings.

Promote Your Videos and Channel: Increase your channel's visibility and reach by actively promoting your videos and channel across social media platforms, your website or blog, and through collaborations with other creators. Greater exposure leads to more views, which in turn increases ad impressions and potential earnings.

Stay Informed and Adapt: The digital advertising landscape is constantly evolving, so it's essential to stay updated on industry trends, changes in ad policies, and new monetization opportunities. Adapt your strategies accordingly to make the most of emerging trends and technologies that can boost your ad revenue and CPM rates.

Engage with Your Audience: Foster a strong connection with your audience by responding to comments, hosting live streams, and creating a sense of community. Engaged viewers are more likely to watch your videos in their entirety, leading to higher ad impressions and CPM rates. Moreover, a loyal and supportive audience can attract brands and advertisers seeking to collaborate with creators who have an active and engaged fan base.

Ad revenue and CPM are vital aspects of YouTube monetization that directly impact your earnings as a content creator. By understanding how these components work and implementing strategies to optimize them, you can unlock the full potential of your channel's earning capabilities. Building a targeted audience, enhancing engagement, improving video quality, experimenting with ad formats, collaborating with brands, optimizing ad placement, utilizing YouTube's monetization features, promoting your videos, staying informed, and engaging with your audience are all key elements in maximizing your ad revenue and CPM rates.

By consistently refining and adapting your approach, you can pave the way to financial success on YouTube and achieve your goal of making millions from your content.

Chapter 12

Exploring Alternative Revenue Streams

YOUTUBE HAS EVOLVED INTO a powerful platform that not only provides entertainment but also offers lucrative opportunities for creators to generate substantial income. While ad revenue is a primary source of earnings for many YouTubers, exploring alternative revenue streams can significantly enhance your financial success. In this chapter, we will delve into various strategies and methods that can help you maximize your earnings on YouTube and potentially make millions.

Affiliate Marketing

Affiliate marketing is a popular and effective way to monetize your YouTube channel. You can make money by working with companies to promote their goods and services and getting paid for each sale or referral made using your special affiliate links. Select products that align with your channel's content and audience to ensure a seamless integration. Engage your viewers with authentic product reviews, tutorials, or recommendations, and provide your affiliate links in the video description or through annotations.

Sponsored Content and Brand Partnerships

Building a strong online presence and a dedicated following can attract potential sponsors and brand collaborations. Many companies are eager to tap into the influence and reach of popular YouTubers to promote their products or services. Negotiating sponsored content deals and brand partnerships can bring in substantial revenue. Ensure that any sponsored content is clearly disclosed to maintain transparency and trust with your audience.

Merchandise and Product Sales

Creating and selling merchandise related to your channel is an excellent way to engage with your audience and generate additional income. Whether it's branded clothing, accessories, or personalized merchandise, fans often love to support their favorite creators by purchasing items they can proudly wear or use. Utilize platforms like Teespring, Shopify, or even create your own online store to sell merchandise directly to your viewers.

Crowdfunding and Fan Donations

If your audience is passionate about your content, they may be willing to contribute financially to support your channel. Platforms like Patreon and Ko-fi enable creators to offer exclusive perks or bonus content to their supporters in exchange for monthly contributions. Additionally, you can consider enabling Super Chat or Super Stickers on live streams, allowing your fans to make donations during the stream. Remember to express your gratitude and acknowledge your supporters to foster a strong sense of community.

Online Courses and Digital Products

Leverage your expertise and knowledge by creating and selling online courses or digital products. If your channel focuses on a specific niche or provides educational content, there is likely an audience interested in learning from you. Develop comprehensive courses or e-books that provide value and offer actionable insights to your viewers. Platforms like Teachable or Udemy can assist in hosting and marketing your courses.

Live Events and Meetups

Organizing live events or meetups can be an exciting way to connect with your audience and monetize your channel. Hosting live shows, workshops, or fan conventions can attract dedicated fans who are willing to purchase tickets to experience your content in person. Additionally, you can collaborate with other creators to create joint events, expanding your reach and revenue potential.

YouTube Premium and Channel Memberships

Joining the YouTube Partner Program and meeting the eligibility criteria allows you to access YouTube's monetization features, including YouTube Premium revenue and channel memberships.

YouTube Premium offers a subscription-based ad-free viewing experience, and as a creator, you can earn a portion of the revenue generated from Premium subscribers. Channel memberships allow you to offer exclusive perks to your subscribers, such as badges, emojis, and access to members-only content, in exchange for a monthly fee.

While ad revenue is an essential component of monetizing your YouTube channel, exploring alternative revenue streams can open up new opportunities for financial success. By strategically implementing strategies like affiliate marketing, sponsored content, merchandise sales, crowdfunding, and digital products, you can maximize your earning potential and potentially make millions from YouTube. Remember, success on YouTube requires dedication, consistency, and delivering high-quality content that resonates with your audience. By diversifying your revenue streams, you can create a stable and sustainable income that goes beyond ad revenue alone.

As you embark on exploring alternative revenue streams, keep these key points in mind:

Understand your audience: Thoroughly research and understand your target audience's interests, needs, and preferences. This knowledge will help you select the most relevant and appealing revenue streams that align with your viewers' preferences.

Maintain authenticity: Your audience is drawn to your channel because of your unique voice and perspective. As you explore different monetization strategies, always maintain authenticity and ensure that any sponsored content or promotional activities align with your channel's values and tone.

Engage with your community: Building a strong and engaged community is vital to your success on YouTube. Regularly interact with your viewers through comments, live streams, and social media platforms. Actively listen to their feedback, respond to their queries, and consider their suggestions when creating new content or introducing new revenue streams.

Continuously improve your content: As the YouTube landscape evolves, it's crucial to adapt and improve your content continually. Stay updated on industry trends, analyze your performance metrics, and experiment with different formats and styles to keep your audience engaged and coming back for more.

Collaborate with other creators: Collaborating with fellow YouTubers can expand your reach, expose you to new audiences, and open doors for potential joint ventures or sponsored collaborations. Seek opportunities to collaborate with creators who share a similar audience or complement your content, providing a win-win situation for both parties.

Market your channel and revenue streams: Developing effective marketing strategies is crucial to gain visibility and attract new viewers and potential customers for your revenue streams. Utilize social media, email marketing, cross-promotion with other platforms, and SEO optimization to increase your channel's visibility and drive traffic to your revenue-generating initiatives.

Remember, making millions from YouTube requires patience, dedication, and continuous effort. Success stories may vary, and it's essential to set realistic expectations while remaining persistent in your pursuit of alternative revenue streams. Be open to adapting your strategies, learning from your experiences, and evolving with the ever-changing digital landscape.

Exploring alternative revenue streams beyond ad revenue is a powerful way to make millions from YouTube. By diversifying your income sources through affiliate marketing, sponsored content, merchandise sales, crowdfunding, digital products, live events, and utilizing YouTube's monetization features, you can significantly enhance your earnings potential.

However, always prioritize the quality and value of your content and maintain an authentic connection with your audience. With determination, creativity, and a comprehensive understanding of your viewers, you can unlock the full potential of YouTube's earning capabilities and pave your way to financial success.

Chapter 13

Sponsorships and Brand Collaborations

IN THIS CHAPTER, WE will delve into the exciting world of sponsorships and brand collaborations. As a YouTube creator, partnering with brands can provide you with lucrative opportunities to monetize your channel and boost your earnings. By creating mutually beneficial relationships with sponsors, you can open doors to a whole new level of financial success on YouTube. In this chapter, we will explore the strategies and best practices to secure sponsorships and brand collaborations that can help you make millions from your YouTube channel.

Understanding Sponsorships

Sponsorships are partnerships between creators and brands where the creator promotes or endorses the brand's products or services. This collaboration often involves a contractual agreement between both parties, outlining the terms and conditions of the partnership. Sponsorships can take various forms, such as product placements, dedicated videos, sponsored segments, brand mentions, or even brand integration within the content.

Building a Solid Foundation

Before approaching brands for sponsorships, it's crucial to build a solid foundation for your channel. This includes having a sizable and engaged audience, consistently producing high-quality content, and establishing your niche or expertise. Brands are more likely to partner with creators who can effectively reach their target audience and provide value through their content. Focus on building your channel's credibility and reputation to attract desirable sponsors.

Researching and Identifying Potential Sponsors

To find the right sponsors for your channel, conduct thorough research. Look for brands that align with your content and resonate with your audience. Consider the products or services that your viewers would be genuinely interested in and explore companies within those industries. Pay attention to the brands already present in your niche and analyze their partnerships with other creators. This will give you insights into potential sponsors who may be interested in collaborating with you.

Crafting an Irresistible Sponsorship Proposal

Once you have identified potential sponsors, it's time to create a compelling sponsorship proposal. Your proposal should showcase the value you can offer to the brand and how your partnership can benefit both parties. Start by introducing yourself and your channel, highlighting your unique selling points and audience demographics. Then, discuss the specific ways you can promote the brand and its products or services. Offer a range of options, such as dedicated videos, sponsored segments, or social media promotions, to cater to different budgets and campaign objectives.

Negotiating the Partnership

When negotiating a sponsorship deal, it's essential to find a balance that benefits both you and the brand. Consider factors such as the scope of work, deliverables, compensation, and exclusivity clauses. Understand the brand's expectations and clearly communicate your own requirements. Discussions about the duration of the partnership, the quantity of sponsored videos, the content usage rights, and the deadline for deliverables may come up during negotiations. Be open to compromise, but also ensure that the terms are fair and align with the value you bring to the table.

Maintaining Authenticity and Transparency

As a YouTube creator, authenticity is crucial to maintaining the trust of your audience. When collaborating with brands, it's important to ensure that the partnership feels genuine and aligns with your content and values. Be transparent with your audience about sponsored content by clearly disclosing when a video is sponsored or contains affiliate links. This transparency will help you maintain the trust you have built with your viewers and prevent any negative backlash.

Delivering Outstanding Results

Once you have secured a sponsorship, it's time to deliver outstanding results. Make sure you fulfill your contractual obligations, meet the agreed-upon deadlines, and provide high-quality content that resonates with your audience. Keep the brand involved throughout the process, sharing progress updates and seeking their feedback to ensure they are satisfied with the collaboration. By exceeding expectations and delivering exceptional results, you increase the chances of building long-term relationships with sponsors and attracting new ones in the future.

Expanding Your Network

While working with sponsors, it's essential to actively expand your network and seek out new opportunities. Attend industry events, conferences, and trade shows to connect with brands, marketers, and other creators. Engage in online communities and platforms specifically designed for creators and brands to foster collaborations. Networking can lead to valuable partnerships and open doors to new sponsorship opportunities that can further enhance your earning potential on YouTube.

Building a Media Kit

A media kit is a powerful tool that showcases your channel's statistics, audience demographics, past collaborations, and achievements. It serves as a professional representation of your brand and can greatly influence potential sponsors. Include relevant information such as your subscriber count, average views per video, engagement rates, and social media following. Additionally, highlight the success of previous sponsorships and the impact they had on the brand's exposure or sales. A well-crafted media kit can make a strong impression and increase your chances of securing sponsorships.

Diversifying Revenue Streams

While sponsorships can be a significant source of income, it's important to diversify your revenue streams to maintain stability and long-term financial success. Explore other monetization methods such as affiliate marketing, merchandise sales, crowdfunding, and brand partnerships outside of YouTube. By diversifying your income, you reduce reliance on a single source and create multiple streams that collectively contribute to your million-dollar goal.

Staying Compliant with FTC Guidelines

The Federal Trade Commission (FTC) has guidelines in place to ensure transparency and protect consumers in sponsored content. It's essential to familiarize yourself with these guidelines and ensure compliance when creating sponsored videos. Clearly disclose your relationship with the brand by using phrases like "This video is sponsored by..." or "Thanks to our sponsor..." prominently in the video or description. Disclose any affiliate links and make sure they are accompanied by a clear explanation to your audience. Staying compliant not only protects you legally but also reinforces trust and transparency with your viewers.

Measuring and Demonstrating ROI

To attract and retain sponsors, it's crucial to measure and demonstrate the return on investment (ROI) they receive from partnering with you. Use analytics tools to track key metrics such as views, engagement, click-through rates, and conversion rates for sponsored content. Analyze the impact of the collaboration on the brand's visibility, sales, or brand perception. Prepare reports and case studies showcasing the success of previous campaigns to illustrate the value you bring to potential sponsors. Demonstrating a positive ROI will make you an attractive partner for brands seeking to maximize their advertising investments.

Sponsorships and brand collaborations have the potential to significantly boost your earnings on YouTube and pave the way to making millions. By building a solid foundation, researching potential sponsors, crafting compelling proposals, and delivering outstanding results, you can secure lucrative partnerships that align with your content and resonate with your audience. Maintain authenticity and transparency, diversify your revenue streams, and stay compliant with FTC guidelines to foster long-term success. Remember, the key to unlocking the full potential of sponsorships lies in creating mutually beneficial relationships that generate value for both you and the brands you partner with.

Chapter 14

Affiliate Marketing on YouTube

IN THIS CHAPTER, WE will explore the lucrative world of affiliate marketing and how it can help you generate substantial income from your YouTube channel. By promoting goods or services and generating purchases through your affiliate links, affiliate marketing presents a special potential to make money. By effectively integrating affiliate marketing into your content strategy, you can leverage your influence and audience to make millions on YouTube. In this chapter, we will delve into the strategies and best practices for successful affiliate marketing on YouTube.

Understanding Affiliate Marketing

Affiliate marketing is a sort of performance-based advertising in which you are compensated for each sale or activity that results from one of your special affiliate links. As a YouTube creator, you can become an affiliate for various companies and promote their products or services to your audience. You receive a share of the sales made when your viewers click on your affiliate links and buy something or finish an action, like joining up for a service.

Choose the Best Affiliate Programmes

When engaging in affiliate marketing, it's essential to pick affiliate programmes that fit your niche and appeal to the audience you want to reach. Research and identify companies that offer products or services your viewers would be genuinely interested in. Take into account the brand's repute, the calibre of their products, and the commission schedule they give. Look for affiliate programs that offer competitive commissions, reliable tracking systems, and comprehensive reporting tools to track your performance effectively.

Integrating Affiliate Links into Your Content

To maximize the effectiveness of affiliate marketing on YouTube, it's important to seamlessly integrate your affiliate links into your content. The key is to make the promotion feel natural and valuable to your viewers. Rather than simply pushing products or services, focus on creating content that educates, entertains, or solves a problem for your audience. Incorporate product reviews, tutorials, "how-to" videos, or demonstrations that showcase the benefits and features of the products or services you're promoting.

Authenticity and Transparency

Maintaining authenticity and transparency is crucial when engaging in affiliate marketing on YouTube. Be honest with your audience about your affiliate partnerships and clearly disclose when a video contains affiliate links. Transparency builds trust and credibility with your viewers, ensuring that they feel informed and empowered to make their own decisions. Focus on providing genuine recommendations and personal experiences with the products or services you promote, as this will resonate more with your audience and increase the likelihood of conversions.

Strategic Placement of Affiliate Links

Strategically placing your affiliate links can significantly impact their visibility and click-through rates. Incorporate your affiliate links within your video descriptions, ensuring they are prominently displayed and easy to find. You can also mention your affiliate links verbally in your videos, encouraging viewers to check out the links in the description box. Additionally, consider using interactive elements such as cards or end screens to direct viewers to your affiliate links. Experiment with different placements and calls-to-action to optimize your conversions.

Tracking and Analyzing Performance

Optimising your affiliate marketing efforts requires tracking and analysing your results. Most affiliate programs provide tracking links or unique identifiers that allow you to monitor the clicks, conversions, and commissions generated through your affiliate links. Leverage analytics tools and reporting dashboards to gain insights into your most successful campaigns, high-converting videos, and top-performing products or services. This data will help you make informed decisions, refine your strategies, and focus on promoting the products or services that resonate most with your audience.

Building Trust through Honest Recommendations

Building audience trust is essential for effective affiliate marketing. Focus on providing honest recommendations and only promoting products or services that you genuinely believe in. By sharing your personal experiences and opinions, you establish credibility and authenticity, which in turn drives your viewers to trust your recommendations. Remember, your audience relies on your expertise and values your honest opinion. It's important to maintain the trust you have built by consistently delivering valuable content and being transparent about your affiliations.

Negotiating Higher Commission Rates

As your YouTube channel grows and your influence increases, you may have the opportunity to negotiate higher commission rates with affiliate programs. If you consistently drive significant sales or conversions for a particular brand, leverage that success to your advantage. Reach out to the affiliate program manager or contact and discuss the possibility of increasing your commission rates. Present them with data and evidence of your performance to showcase the value you bring to their program. Negotiating higher commission rates can significantly boost your earnings from affiliate marketing.

Diversifying Affiliate Programs and Products

To maximize your earnings from affiliate marketing, it's beneficial to diversify your affiliate programs and the range of products or services you promote. Explore multiple affiliate networks and platforms to find a variety of programs that align with your content and audience. This diversification spreads the risk and ensures that you have multiple income streams from different sources. Additionally, promoting a wide range of products or services allows you to cater to different preferences and needs within your audience, increasing the chances of conversions.

Continuously Testing and Optimizing

Successful affiliate marketing requires continuous testing, optimization, and adaptation. To learn what appeals to your audience the most, test out various advertising tactics, content structures, and product offerings. A/B test different calls-to-action, video titles, thumbnail images, and affiliate link placements to determine what drives the highest click-through and conversion rates. Monitor your analytics and adjust your approach accordingly, focusing on the strategies and products that yield the best results.

Expanding Beyond YouTube

While YouTube is an excellent platform for affiliate marketing, consider expanding your reach beyond YouTube to further maximize your earnings. Leverage your social media presence by sharing affiliate links on platforms like Instagram, Twitter, Facebook, or TikTok. Create blog posts or articles that include your affiliate links and drive traffic to your website. By diversifying your promotional channels, you can tap into different audiences and increase your chances of generating sales and commissions.

Building Long-Term Relationships

Establishing long-term relationships with affiliate programs and brands can be highly beneficial. By consistently delivering results and providing value, you can position yourself as a trusted partner and increase your opportunities for exclusive offers, higher commission rates, or early access to new products. Maintain open communication with affiliate program managers, provide feedback on product performance, and collaborate on future promotional campaigns. Building long-term relationships can lead to ongoing revenue streams and continuous growth in your affiliate marketing endeavors.

Affiliate marketing is a powerful monetization strategy that can help you make millions from your YouTube channel. By choosing the right affiliate programs, seamlessly integrating affiliate links into your content, maintaining authenticity and transparency, strategically placing links, tracking and analyzing performance, and continuously optimizing your strategies, you can unlock the full potential of affiliate marketing on YouTube.

Remember, success lies in building trust with your audience, providing valuable recommendations, and diversifying your affiliate programs and products. With dedication, experimentation, and a strong focus on delivering value, you can achieve substantial financial success through affiliate marketing on YouTube.

Chapter 15

Merchandise and Product Sale

In this chapter, we'll dive into the exciting world of merchandise and product sales, exploring how YouTubers can leverage their brand and audience to create profitable revenue streams beyond ad revenue alone. By strategically developing and selling merchandise, you can not only increase your income but also engage with your loyal fanbase on a whole new level. So, let's get started and discover how you can turn your YouTube channel into a thriving merchandise business.

Building Your Brand

Before delving into merchandise sales, it's crucial to establish a strong and recognizable brand for your YouTube channel. Your brand identity should align with your content and resonate with your target audience. Take the time to define your niche, understand your viewers' preferences, and develop a cohesive brand strategy. A well-defined brand will serve as the foundation for successful merchandise sales.

Understanding Your Audience

To create merchandise that sells, it's essential to understand your audience's interests, preferences, and demographics. Analyze your YouTube analytics to gain insights into your viewers' demographics, including age, gender, and location. Additionally, engage with your audience through comments, social media, and community posts to get a sense of their likes and dislikes. This knowledge will guide you in designing merchandise that appeals to your fanbase and maximizes sales potential.

Designing Merchandise

When it comes to merchandise design, creativity is key. Your merchandise should reflect your brand and resonate with your audience. Consider incorporating your logo, catchphrases, or inside jokes from your videos into your designs. Collaborating with professional designers or seeking input from your community can yield fresh and unique ideas.

Ensure that your merchandise is of high quality. Whether it's t-shirts, hoodies, mugs, or phone cases, invest in products that are durable, comfortable, and visually appealing. The quality of your merchandise reflects on your brand, and satisfied customers are more likely to become repeat buyers and brand ambassadors.

Setting Up an Online Store

To sell your merchandise effectively, you need a well-designed and user-friendly online store. Several e-commerce platforms, such as Shopify, WooCommerce, or BigCommerce, offer easy-to-use templates and customizable options to create your store. Consider integrating your online store with your YouTube channel and social media platforms to provide a seamless shopping experience for your audience.

Product Pricing

Determining the right price for your merchandise requires careful consideration. Consider the production costs, including manufacturing, packaging, and shipping. Take into account your profit margin and market demand. Research similar products in your niche and analyze their pricing strategies. Aim for a balance between affordability and profitability, ensuring that your audience perceives value in your merchandise.

Promoting Your Merchandise

Effective promotion is essential for driving merchandise sales. Leverage your YouTube channel, social media platforms, and other online marketing channels to create buzz around your products. Here are a few strategies to consider:

Video Promotions: Create engaging videos showcasing your merchandise. Highlight its features, explain its benefits, and share personal anecdotes about its significance. Encourage your audience to purchase and support your channel.

Collaborations: Collaborate with other YouTubers, influencers, or brands to cross-promote merchandise. This can expose your products to a broader audience and generate additional sales.

Limited Editions and Exclusive Drops: Create a sense of urgency and exclusivity by releasing limited-edition merchandise or announcing surprise drops. This strategy can generate excitement and drive impulse purchases.

Contests and Giveaways: Organize contests or giveaways where viewers can win your merchandise. This not only encourages engagement but also creates brand awareness and loyalty.

Email Marketing: Build an email list of your most loyal subscribers and send them exclusive offer discounts, or early access to new merchandise. Email marketing allows you to directly communicate with your dedicated fanbase and incentivize them to make purchases.

Social Media Advertising: Utilize targeted social media advertising to reach a wider audience. Platforms like Facebook, Instagram, and Twitter offer advanced targeting options that allow you to reach users who have similar interests to your channel's niche.

Customer Service and Fulfillment

In order to establish a good reputation and promote clients to return, outstanding customer service is essential. Ensure that your customers have a seamless purchasing experience by offering multiple payment options, a secure checkout process, and clear product descriptions. Respond promptly to customer inquiries, address any concerns or issues, and strive for quick and reliable shipping.

Consider partnering with a reputable fulfillment company to handle inventory management, packaging, and shipping. This can save you time and ensure that orders are processed efficiently. Research fulfillment options that align with your budget and geographic reach, ensuring that your merchandise reaches customers worldwide.

Engaging with Your Community

Merchandise sales present a unique opportunity to engage with your community on a deeper level. Encourage your fans to share photos or videos of themselves wearing or using your merchandise and feature them on your social media platforms or in your videos. Organize meetups, fan events, or conventions where your audience can connect with you and each other, fostering a sense of belonging and community.

Monitoring and Adapting

Continuously monitor the performance of your merchandise sales. Analyze sales data, customer feedback, and market trends to identify what products are resonating with your audience and what can be improved. Use this information to refine your merchandise offerings, introduce new designs or products, and stay ahead of the curve.

Protecting Your Brand

As your merchandise business grows, it becomes essential to protect your brand and intellectual property. Consider trademarking your brand name, logo, and any unique designs to prevent unauthorized use. Stay vigilant for counterfeit merchandise and take appropriate action to protect your customers and maintain the integrity of your brand.

Merchandise and product sales offer YouTube creators an exciting opportunity to expand their revenue streams and deepen their connection with their audience. By building a strong brand, understanding your audience, designing high-quality merchandise, and implementing effective promotion strategies, you can create a successful merchandise business alongside your YouTube channel.

Remember, building a merchandise business takes time, effort, and a commitment to providing value to your audience. Stay focused, listen to your community, and adapt your strategies as needed. With dedication and creativity, you can turn your YouTube channel into a lucrative brand that extends beyond the screen and into the lives of your fans.

Part III
Growing Your YouTube Channel

Chapter 16

Engaging with Your Audience

BY THIS POINT IN the book, you've learned the ins and outs of creating captivating content, optimizing your channel, and monetizing your YouTube videos. But there's one crucial aspect that can make or break your success as a YouTuber: engaging with your audience. Building a strong connection with your viewers is the key to establishing a loyal fanbase, growing your channel, and ultimately making millions from YouTube. In this chapter, we'll dive deep into the strategies and techniques you can use to effectively engage with your audience and create a thriving YouTube community.

Respond to Comments: The comment section is the heart of audience engagement on YouTube. Make it a priority to respond to as many comments as possible, showing your viewers that you value their input and appreciate their support. Take the time to address their questions, acknowledge their opinions, and offer genuine responses. Engaging with your audience in the comment section will make them feel heard and connected to you, fostering a sense of community.

Ask for Feedback: Actively seek feedback from your audience. This can be done through video content, social media posts, or even dedicated feedback surveys. Encourage your viewers to share their thoughts, suggestions, and ideas for future videos. Not only does this give your audience a sense of ownership, but it also allows you to tailor your content to their preferences, increasing the chances of attracting and retaining loyal subscribers.

Live Interaction: Hosting live streams or Q&A sessions is an excellent way to engage with your audience in real-time. These interactive sessions allow you to directly connect with your viewers, answer their questions, and address their concerns. Live streaming fosters a sense of intimacy and authenticity, as your audience gets to see the real you, unfiltered and unscripted. Make sure to promote these live events well in advance to maximize attendance.

Collaborate with Viewers: Involve your audience in your content creation process by collaborating with them. You can hold contests, challenges, or even invite viewers to contribute ideas, artwork, or video clips. By including your audience in your videos, you not only strengthen the bond between you and your viewers but also give them a chance to showcase their talents and be part of something bigger.

Utilize Social Media: Leverage the power of social media platforms to engage with your audience beyond YouTube. Create accounts on platforms like Instagram, Twitter, and Facebook, and actively engage with your followers there. Share behind-the-scenes content, sneak peeks, and personal updates to provide an exclusive experience for your fans. Engage in conversations, reply to comments, and share content from your followers to foster a sense of community and gratitude.

Attend Events and Meetups: Whenever possible, participate in YouTube-related events, conferences, or fan meetups. These gatherings offer a unique opportunity to connect with your audience face-to-face, strengthening the personal bond you've built online. Interacting with your viewers in person can leave a lasting impression and create powerful advocates for your channel. Remember to promote your attendance in advance to ensure maximum turnout.

Create Exclusive Content: Reward your most dedicated fans with exclusive content that is not available to the general public. This can be in the form of bonus videos, early access to content, or special merchandise. By providing these perks, you make your audience feel special and appreciated, cultivating a sense of loyalty and commitment.

Show Appreciation: Expressing gratitude towards your audience goes a long way in building a strong connection. Take the time to thank your viewers in your videos, give shoutouts to loyal subscribers, or even feature fan-made content in your videos. Small gestures like these can make your audience feel valued and acknowledged, fostering a deeper sense of community and support.

Analyze and Implement Viewer Data: Take advantage of YouTube analytics to gain insights into your audience's preferences, demographics, and viewing habits. Use this data to inform your content creation decisions, making sure you cater to your audience's interests. By tailoring your content to what your viewers want, you'll increase engagement, attract more subscribers, and boost your overall success.

Stay Consistent: Consistency is key when it comes to engaging with your audience. Regularly upload videos, maintain a consistent tone, and respond promptly to comments and messages. Being dependable and predictable helps you establish trust with your audience, increasing the likelihood that they will interact with your content and stick with you.

Remember, engaging with your audience is an ongoing process that requires dedication, authenticity, and genuine care. By implementing the strategies outlined in this chapter and adapting them to your unique style and audience, you'll foster a thriving YouTube community that will support you on your journey to making millions from YouTube.

Chapter 17

Utilizing Social Media to Promote Your Channel

IN TODAY'S DIGITAL AGE, social media has become an integral part of our lives. It has revolutionized the way we connect and communicate with others, making it a powerful tool for promoting your YouTube channel. Leveraging social media platforms to enhance your channel's visibility and reach is a smart strategy that can significantly boost your chances of success. In this chapter, we will explore effective techniques and strategies to utilize social media to promote your YouTube channel and ultimately help you make millions.

Create Engaging Social Media Profiles:

To effectively promote your YouTube channel on social media, you need to create compelling and visually appealing profiles. Optimize your profile descriptions with relevant keywords and include a link to your YouTube channel. Use high-quality profile pictures and cover photos that align with your brand. Consistency in branding across platforms helps create a cohesive and recognizable presence.

Cross-Promote Content:

One of the most effective ways to promote your YouTube channel on social media is through cross-promotion. Share teasers, trailers, or snippets of your YouTube videos on platforms like Instagram, Twitter, and Facebook. Create engaging captions or headlines that entice viewers to watch the full video on your channel. This cross-promotion technique can drive traffic from social media to your YouTube videos, increasing views and subscribers.

Leverage Video Thumbnails:

Social media platforms often display video thumbnails to capture users' attention. Design eye-catching and clickable thumbnails for your YouTube videos. Highlight the main topic or a captivating moment to intrigue potential viewers. Use bold text, bright colors, and high-resolution images to create visually appealing thumbnails that stand out in crowded feeds. Remember, a compelling thumbnail can significantly impact click-through rates.

Social media is all about building relationships and engaging with your audience. Respond to comments, messages, and mentions promptly. Encourage discussions, ask for feedback, and appreciate your viewers' support. By actively participating in conversations and showing genuine interest, you create a loyal community around your channel. This not only enhances your channel's reputation but also attracts new viewers.

Hashtags and Trending Topics:

Harness the power of hashtags and trending topics on social media to increase your channel's visibility. To attract a larger audience on social media, do some research and include suitable hashtags to your postings. Stay updated with the latest trends and incorporate them into your content when appropriate. By leveraging popular hashtags and trending topics, you can tap into ongoing conversations and expose your YouTube channel to a broader audience.

Collaborate with Influencers:

Influencer marketing has become a potent force in social media promotion. Identify influencers within your niche who have a substantial following and engage with them. Collaborate on projects, feature each other's content, or co-create videos. These partnerships can expose your channel to a new audience and generate valuable cross-promotion opportunities. Be sure to choose influencers whose values align with your brand for authentic collaborations.

Live Streaming and Q&A Sessions:

Live streaming has gained immense popularity across various social media platforms. Utilize this feature to interact with your audience in real-time, host Q&A sessions, or share behind-the-scenes content. Promote your live stream in advance on social media to generate excitement and maximize attendance.

Run Social Media Contests:

Contests and giveaways are excellent ways to generate buzz and engage your audience on social media. Organize contests where viewers can participate by liking, sharing, or commenting on your posts. Offer enticing prizes related to your channel's niche to attract relevant participants. Encourage participants to subscribe to your YouTube channel for additional entries. Contests not only increase your channel's visibility but also create a sense of excitement and reward for your loyal viewers.

Advertise on Social Media:

Social media platforms offer powerful advertising tools that can further enhance your YouTube channel's promotion. Utilize the targeting options provided by platforms like Facebook Ads or Instagram Ads to reach your specific audience. Create compelling ad campaigns with captivating visuals and concise messaging to entice users to click and discover your channel. Set a budget and monitor the performance of your ads to ensure optimal results.

Incorporating social media into your YouTube channel promotion strategy is a must in today's digital landscape. By leveraging the power of social media platforms, you can significantly increase your channel's visibility, reach, and ultimately, your chances of making millions.

Remember to create engaging profiles, cross-promote content, engage with your audience, leverage hashtags and trending topics, collaborate with influencers, utilize live streaming, run contests, and consider social media advertising. With a well-rounded social media strategy, you can propel your YouTube channel to new heights of success.

Chapter 18

Cross-Promotion and Collaboration Strategies

In the ever-evolving world of YouTube, standing out from the crowd and gaining a substantial following can be a challenging endeavor. However, one of the most effective ways to accelerate your growth and maximize your earnings is through cross-promotion and collaboration strategies. By teaming up with other content creators, you can tap into new audiences, expand your reach, and build mutually beneficial relationships. In this chapter, we will delve into the art of cross-promotion and collaboration on YouTube and explore various strategies that can help you make millions.

The Power of Collaboration:

Collaboration is the secret ingredient that can propel your channel to new heights. By joining forces with like-minded creators, you can combine your strengths, share your audiences, and create content that is greater than the sum of its parts. Collaborations offer several benefits, including increased visibility, access to new viewers, and the potential for exponential growth. They also provide opportunities to learn from others, exchange ideas, and build lasting connections within the YouTube community.

Choosing the Right Collaborators:

When it comes to selecting collaborators, it's essential to find creators whose content aligns with yours and whose audience demographics complement your own. Look for individuals who share your values, have a similar subscriber count, and possess a genuine interest in working together. Research potential collaborators thoroughly to ensure they have a good reputation and a track record of producing quality content. Remember, the success of your collaboration relies heavily on the chemistry and synergy between both parties.

Types of Collaborative Content:

There are various ways to approach collaboration on YouTube, each offering its unique benefits. Some popular forms of collaborative content include:

a) Guest Appearances: Inviting a guest creator to appear on your channel or vice versa can introduce both audiences to new content and foster cross-promotion. This can take the form of interviews, discussions, or even joint challenges.

b) Collaborative Projects: Collaborating on a project, such as a series or a mini-documentary, can create excitement and anticipation among your viewers. This type of collaboration allows both creators to contribute their expertise, creating a rich and engaging experience for the audience.

c) Cross-Promotion: Another effective strategy is cross-promotion, where creators promote each other's channels or videos within their own content. This can be done through shout-outs, end-screen annotations, or even dedicated promotional videos.

Planning and Executing Collaborations:

Successful collaborations require careful planning and execution. Here are some steps to consider when embarking on a collaborative venture:

a) Set Clear Goals: Clearly define your objectives for the collaboration. Are you looking to expand your audience, increase subscribers, or explore new content genres? Aligning your goals with your collaborator's goals will ensure a mutually beneficial experience.

b) Establish Roles and Responsibilities: Assign specific roles and responsibilities to each collaborator to ensure a smooth workflow. This includes determining who will handle pre-production tasks, filming, editing, and promotional efforts.

c) Create a Content Plan: Develop a comprehensive content plan that leverages the strengths of both collaborators. Brainstorm ideas, outline the structure of the content, and establish a timeline for production and release.

d) Communicate Effectively: Maintain open lines of communication throughout the collaboration process. Regularly discuss ideas, address any concerns, and make sure both parties are on the same page. A collaborative effort thrives on effective communication and mutual understanding.

e) Leverage Cross-Promotion: Utilize cross-promotion techniques to maximize the impact of your collaboration. Feature your collaborator's channel and content prominently within your videos and encourage your viewers to check out their content. In turn, your collaborator should reciprocate the cross-promotion efforts.

Post-Collaboration Strategies:

The collaboration doesn't end once the content is released. It's crucial to leverage the momentum generated from the collaboration and implement post-collaboration strategies to continue reaping the benefits. Here are some post-collaboration strategies to consider:

a) Engage with Viewers: Encourage your viewers to share their thoughts and feedback on the collaboration. Respond to comments, engage in discussions, and show appreciation for their support. This interaction will help strengthen your connection with your audience.

b) Analyze Performance: Monitor the performance of the collaboration through analytics and data. Assess the impact on metrics such as views, subscribers, engagement, and watch time. Identify what worked well and areas for improvement, allowing you to refine your future collaboration strategies.

c) Follow-up Collaborations: If the collaboration was successful, consider exploring further collaborative opportunities with the same creator or others in your niche. Building a network of collaborators can create a snowball effect, leading to increased exposure and growth for all parties involved.

d) Maintain Relationships: After the collaboration, it's essential to maintain relationships with your collaborators. Support their future endeavors, engage with their content, and continue to cross-promote each other. Nurturing these connections can lead to future collaborations and ongoing mutual benefits.

Cross-promotion and collaboration strategies have the potential to revolutionize your YouTube channel, driving substantial growth and financial success. By harnessing the power of collaboration, carefully selecting the right collaborators, and implementing effective strategies, you can expand your reach, tap into new audiences, and unlock new opportunities. Remember, collaboration is not just about boosting your numbers; it's about building genuine relationships, fostering creativity, and creating content that resonates with viewers. Embrace collaboration as a powerful tool in your journey towards making millions on YouTube.

Chapter 18

Cross-Promotion and Collaboration Strategies

In the ever-evolving world of YouTube, standing out from the crowd and gaining a substantial following can be a challenging endeavor. However, one of the most effective ways to accelerate your growth and maximize your earnings is through cross-promotion and collaboration strategies. By teaming up with other content creators, you can tap into new audiences, expand your reach, and build mutually beneficial relationships. In this chapter, we will delve into the art of cross-promotion and collaboration on YouTube and explore various strategies that can help you make millions.

The Power of Collaboration:

Collaboration is the secret ingredient that can propel your channel to new heights. By joining forces with like-minded creators, you can combine your strengths, share your audiences, and create content that is greater than the sum of its parts. Collaborations offer several benefits, including increased visibility, access to new viewers, and the potential for exponential growth. They also provide opportunities to learn from others, exchange ideas, and build lasting connections within the YouTube community.

Choosing the Right Collaborators:

When it comes to selecting collaborators, it's essential to find creators whose content aligns with yours and whose audience demographics complement your own. Look for individuals who share your values, have a similar subscriber count, and possess a genuine interest in working together. Research potential collaborators thoroughly to ensure they have a good reputation and a track record of producing quality content. Remember, the success of your collaboration relies heavily on the chemistry and synergy between both parties.

Types of Collaborative Content:

There are various ways to approach collaboration on YouTube, each offering its unique benefits. Some popular forms of collaborative content include:

a) Guest Appearances: Inviting a guest creator to appear on your channel or vice versa can introduce both audiences to new content and foster cross-promotion. This can take the form of interviews, discussions, or even joint challenges.

b) Collaborative Projects: Collaborating on a project, such as a series or a mini-documentary, can create excitement and anticipation among your viewers. This type of collaboration allows both creators to contribute their expertise, creating a rich and engaging experience for the audience.

c) Cross-Promotion: Another effective strategy is cross-promotion, where creators promote each other's channels or videos within their own content. This can be done through shout-outs, end-screen annotations, or even dedicated promotional videos.

Planning and Executing Collaborations:

Successful collaborations require careful planning and execution. Here are some steps to consider when embarking on a collaborative venture:

a) Set Clear Goals: Clearly define your objectives for the collaboration. Are you looking to expand your audience, increase subscribers, or explore new content genres? Aligning your goals with your collaborator's goals will ensure a mutually beneficial experience.

b) Establish Roles and Responsibilities: Assign specific roles and responsibilities to each collaborator to ensure a smooth workflow. This includes determining who will handle pre-production tasks, filming, editing, and promotional efforts.

c) Create a Content Plan: Develop a comprehensive content plan that leverages the strengths of both collaborators. Brainstorm ideas, outline the structure of the content, and establish a timeline for production and release.

d) Communicate Effectively: Maintain open lines of communication throughout the collaboration process. Regularly discuss ideas, address any concerns, and make sure both parties are on the same page. A collaborative effort thrives on effective communication and mutual understanding.

e) Leverage Cross-Promotion: Utilize cross-promotion techniques to maximize the impact of your collaboration. Feature your collaborator's channel and content prominently within your videos and encourage your viewers to check out their content. In turn, your collaborator should reciprocate the cross-promotion efforts.

Post-Collaboration Strategies:

The collaboration doesn't end once the content is released. It's crucial to leverage the momentum generated from the collaboration and implement post-collaboration strategies to continue reaping the benefits. Here are some post-collaboration strategies to consider:

a) Engage with Viewers: Encourage your viewers to share their thoughts and feedback on the collaboration. Respond to comments, engage in discussions, and show appreciation for their support. This interaction will help strengthen your connection with your audience.

b) Analyze Performance: Monitor the performance of the collaboration through analytics and data. Assess the impact on metrics such as views, subscribers, engagement, and watch time. Identify what worked well and areas for improvement, allowing you to refine your future collaboration strategies.

c) Follow-up Collaborations: If the collaboration was successful, consider exploring further collaborative opportunities with the same creator or others in your niche. Building a network of collaborators can create a snowball effect, leading to increased exposure and growth for all parties involved.

d) Maintain Relationships: After the collaboration, it's essential to maintain relationships with your collaborators. Support their future endeavors, engage with their content, and continue to cross-promote each other. Nurturing these connections can lead to future collaborations and ongoing mutual benefits.

Cross-promotion and collaboration strategies have the potential to revolutionize your YouTube channel, driving substantial growth and financial success. By harnessing the power of collaboration, carefully selecting the right collaborators, and implementing effective strategies, you can expand your reach, tap into new audiences, and unlock new opportunities. Remember, collaboration is not just about boosting your numbers; it's about building genuine relationships, fostering creativity, and creating content that resonates with viewers. Embrace collaboration as a powerful tool in your journey towards making millions on YouTube.

Chapter 19

YouTube SEO and Algorithm Optimization

IN THE COMPETITIVE LANDSCAPE of YouTube, having exceptional content is just the first step towards success. To truly make millions from YouTube, you need to understand the intricacies of YouTube's search engine optimization (SEO) and algorithm optimization. By strategically optimizing your videos and channel to align with YouTube's algorithms, you can increase your visibility, attract more viewers, and ultimately boost your earnings. In this chapter, we will delve into the world of YouTube SEO and algorithm optimization, exploring effective strategies that will give you a competitive edge.

Understanding YouTube's Algorithm:

YouTube's algorithm is a complex system that determines which videos are displayed to users and in what order. Although the exact workings of the algorithm are closely guarded secrets, understanding the key factors that influence it can help you optimize your content effectively. Some crucial elements of YouTube's algorithm include:

a) Relevance: YouTube aims to deliver the most relevant content to its users. The algorithm considers factors such as video titles, descriptions, tags, and viewer engagement to determine relevance.

b) Engagement: Viewer engagement plays a vital role in YouTube's algorithm. Metrics like watch time, likes, comments, shares, and subscriptions signal to the algorithm that your content is valuable and deserving of promotion.

c) Retention: YouTube prioritizes videos that keep viewers engaged for longer durations. High watch time and audience retention indicate quality content that should be recommended to a broader audience.

d) Click-through Rate (CTR): The CTR is the percentage of users who click on your video after seeing it in search results or suggested videos. A high CTR suggests that your video's title, thumbnail, and metadata are compelling and relevant to users' interests.

Keyword Research and Optimization:

Keyword research is a critical component of YouTube SEO. By identifying the right keywords and incorporating them strategically into your content, you can improve your video's visibility and reach. Here's how to approach keyword research and optimization:

a) Research Popular Keywords: Use keyword research tools like Google Keyword Planner, TubeBuddy, or VidIQ to identify popular and relevant keywords in your niche. Look for keywords with a high search volume but manageable competition.

b) Optimize Video Titles: Craft catchy and descriptive video titles that include your target keywords. Keep the title concise, compelling, and easy to understand.

c) Write Detailed Descriptions: Utilize the video description section to provide a comprehensive summary of your video. Include relevant keywords naturally within the description while maintaining readability.

d) Tag Appropriately: Choose relevant tags that accurately represent the content of your video. Incorporate a mix of broad and specific tags to increase your chances of appearing in search results.

e) Thumbnail Optimization: Design visually appealing and compelling thumbnails that accurately represent your video's content. Use text overlays, vibrant colors, and high-quality images to catch viewers' attention.

Engaging and Retaining Viewers:

YouTube's algorithm rewards videos that captivate and retain viewers. Here are some ways to keep your audience interested and attentive:

a) **Hook Viewers Early:** Capture viewers' attention within the first few seconds of your video. Use an intriguing hook, captivating visuals, or a compelling question to pique their curiosity and encourage them to continue watching.

b) **Provide Value**: Deliver valuable content that aligns with viewers' expectations. Understand your audience's interests and needs, and create videos that offer solutions, information, entertainment, or inspiration.

c) **Improve Video Quality:** Invest in good equipment, lighting, and sound to enhance the overall production quality of your videos. High-quality videos are more likely to captivate viewers and keep them engaged.

d) **Optimize Video Length:** Consider the optimal video length for your content. While it varies depending on your niche and audience preferences, strive to provide valuable information within a reasonable timeframe. Longer videos should have a compelling structure and pacing to maintain viewer interest.

e) **Encourage Interaction:** Encourage viewers to engage with your content by asking questions, seeking opinions, or inviting comments. Respond to comments promptly and foster a sense of community on your channel.

Building Channel Authority:

Building authority and credibility in your niche can significantly impact your video's visibility and discoverability. Here's how to establish your channel as an authoritative source:

a) Consistency is Key: Maintain a consistent upload schedule to demonstrate reliability and build anticipation among your audience. Regularly releasing quality content helps establish your channel's authority.

b) Playlists and Series: Organize your videos into playlists and create series that tackle specific topics. This not only makes it easier for viewers to navigate your content but also signals to YouTube that your channel offers comprehensive and valuable information.

c) Collaborations with Influencers: Collaborating with established influencers or experts in your niche can help you tap into their audience and enhance your credibility. By associating with respected creators, you can gain exposure and attract new viewers.

d) Cross-Promotion: Actively promote your videos and channel on other platforms, such as social media, blogs, or podcasts. Leverage your existing network and seek opportunities for cross-promotion with complementary content creators.

e) Engage with Your Community: Foster a sense of community on your channel by responding to comments, holding Q&A sessions, or creating dedicated content based on viewer suggestions. Engaging with your audience builds loyalty and strengthens your channel's authority.

Mastering YouTube SEO and algorithm optimization is essential for maximizing your earning potential on the platform. By understanding the factors that influence YouTube's algorithm, conducting thorough keyword research, engaging and retaining viewers, and building channel authority, you can position yourself for success. Remember, YouTube's algorithms are constantly evolving, so it's crucial to stay updated on the latest trends and best practices. By continuously refining your SEO strategies, you can gain a competitive edge and pave the way to making millions from YouTube.

Chapter 20

Analyzing Analytics and Insights

WELCOME TO CHAPTER 20 of "How to Make Millions from YouTube." In this chapter, we will dive deep into the world of analytics and insights, and explore how you can leverage them to maximize your success on YouTube. Analytics and insights are invaluable tools that provide you with a wealth of data about your channel and audience, enabling you to make informed decisions, optimize your content strategy, and ultimately grow your channel into a lucrative business.

Understanding YouTube Analytics

YouTube Analytics is a powerful tool provided by the platform itself, offering a comprehensive overview of your channel's performance. It provides you with detailed information on key metrics such as views, watch time, subscribers, engagement, and revenue. By understanding and analyzing these metrics, you can gain insights into your audience's behavior and preferences, allowing you to tailor your content to their needs.

Views and Watch Time

Views and watch time are fundamental metrics that indicate how many people are watching your videos and how long they are engaged with your content. Monitoring these metrics can help you understand which videos are performing well and attracting a larger audience. It's important to analyze the watch time specifically, as it is a crucial factor in YouTube's algorithm, which determines the visibility of your videos. Creating engaging and longer videos can help boost your watch time, leading to higher rankings and increased exposure.

Subscribers and Engagement

The number of subscribers and the level of engagement on your channel are key indicators of your overall success. Subscribers represent your loyal fan base, and their support can greatly impact the growth of your channel. Analyzing the subscriber count over time can provide insights into the effectiveness of your content and marketing strategies. Furthermore, tracking metrics such as likes, comments, and shares can help you gauge the level of engagement and the resonance of your content with your audience.

Demographics and Audience Insights

Understanding your audience is essential for tailoring your content to their preferences. YouTube Analytics offers valuable demographic information, including the age, gender, and geographic location of your viewers. Analyzing this data can help you identify your target audience, allowing you to create content that resonates with them. Additionally, YouTube Analytics provides audience retention metrics, which show how engaged your viewers are at different points in your videos. By examining this data, you can identify patterns and make adjustments to optimize your content for maximum retention.

Traffic Sources and Discovery

YouTube Analytics provides insights into how viewers discover your videos. It breaks down your traffic sources into various categories, such as YouTube search, suggested videos, external websites, and social media platforms. Analyzing these sources can help you understand which channels or platforms are driving traffic to your videos. This knowledge allows you to focus your promotional efforts on the most effective channels and optimize your content for better visibility within the YouTube ecosystem.

Revenue Generation and Monetization

For many creators, YouTube is not just a passion but also a source of income. YouTube Analytics provides valuable data on your channel's revenue generation, including AdSense earnings, YouTube Premium revenue, and Super Chat revenue. Analyzing this data can help you identify trends, understand the impact of different monetization strategies, and optimize your revenue streams. By identifying which videos or content types generate the most revenue, you can make informed decisions about your content creation and monetization strategies.

Utilizing Third-Party Analytics Tools

While YouTube Analytics provides comprehensive data about your channel's performance, there are also third-party analytics tools that can further enhance your analysis. Tools like Google Analytics and Social Blade offer additional insights and metrics that can provide a more holistic view of your channel's performance. These tools can help you track external traffic, analyze audience behavior on your website or other social media platforms, and identify opportunities for collaboration or sponsorships.

Iterating and Optimizing Your Content Strategy

Analyzing analytics and insights is not a one-time task; it's an ongoing process that requires continuous monitoring and adaptation. By regularly reviewing your data and identifying patterns, you can refine your content strategy and make data-driven decisions. Experimenting with different formats, topics, and styles based on the insights gained from analytics can help you attract and retain a larger audience. Additionally, keeping an eye on trends and staying up to date with the ever-evolving YouTube landscape can give you a competitive edge and help you capitalize on emerging opportunities.

In this chapter, we explored the world of analytics and insights on YouTube. We discussed the importance of understanding YouTube

Analytics and its various metrics, including views, watch time, subscribers, engagement, demographics, traffic sources, and revenue generation. We also touched on the significance of third-party analytics tools and the need for continuous iteration and optimization of your content strategy based on the insights gained.

By leveraging analytics and insights effectively, you can make informed decisions, drive growth, and ultimately transform your YouTube channel into a thriving business. Remember, data is power, so embrace it and let it guide you toward millions on YouTube.

Chapter 21

Understanding Trending Topics and Viral Content

IN THIS CHAPTER, WE will delve into the fascinating world of trending topics and viral content. Understanding and leveraging these phenomena can be a game-changer for your YouTube channel, as they have the potential to skyrocket your views, engagement, and ultimately, your revenue. In this chapter, we will explore the strategies and techniques you can employ to identify trending topics, create viral content, and capitalize on the immense opportunities they present.

The Power of Trending Topics

Trending topics are subjects or themes that gain significant attention and popularity within a specific period. They can range from current events, news stories, viral challenges, to cultural phenomena and pop culture references. Leveraging trending topics allows you to tap into existing conversations and capitalize on the increased search volume and viewership associated with them. By incorporating these topics into your content, you can attract a wider audience, increase engagement, and position yourself as a relevant and timely creator.

Identifying Trending Topics

Staying on top of trending topics requires a proactive approach to monitoring news, social media, and popular culture. Here are a few strategies to help you identify and capitalize on trending topics:

Stay Informed: Keep yourself updated on current events, news stories, and popular culture by regularly consuming news sources, following influential figures and organizations on social media, and engaging in relevant communities and forums. This will help you identify emerging trends and topics that have the potential to go viral.

Use Online Tools: There are various online tools and platforms available that can help you identify trending topics. Social media platforms like Twitter and Facebook have dedicated sections that highlight trending topics based on their popularity and engagement. Additionally, tools like Google Trends and Buzzsumo provide insights into the most searched and shared topics across different categories and regions.

Follow Industry Influencers: Influencers and thought leaders within your niche often have their finger on the pulse of trending topics. By following and engaging with them, you can gain valuable insights and inspiration for creating content around relevant and popular subjects.

Creating Viral Content

It takes a special kind of imagination, timing, and strategic thought to produce viral content. While there is no guaranteed formula for creating viral content, there are certain elements and strategies that can increase your chances of success:

Emotionally Resonant Content: Viral content often elicits strong emotional reactions from viewers. Whether it's humor, awe, inspiration, or surprise, tapping into emotions can make your content more shareable and increase its virality. Consider incorporating storytelling techniques, relatable anecdotes, or compelling visuals to evoke emotions in your audience.

Unique and Original Ideas: Standing out in a sea of content requires uniqueness and originality. Find ways to present your content from a fresh perspective, introduce innovative concepts, or offer a unique spin on popular topics. This will capture the attention of viewers and make your content more likely to be shared and talked about.

Engaging Thumbnails and Titles: Thumbnails and titles are the first impressions viewers have of your content. Creating attention-grabbing thumbnails that accurately represent your video and crafting compelling titles can significantly increase click-through rates. Be sure to use eye-catching visuals, clear text, and incorporate relevant keywords to optimize searchability.

Ride the Wave: Sometimes, creating viral content involves capitalizing on existing trends or challenges. By participating in popular challenges, creating reaction videos, or providing commentary on trending topics, you can piggyback on the existing buzz and increase your chances of going viral.

Promoting Viral Content

Creating viral content is only half the battle; promoting it effectively is equally important. Here are some strategies to help you promote your viral content and maximize its reach:

Optimize for SEO: Implementing search engine optimization (SEO) techniques can help your content rank higher in search results and increase its visibility. Conduct keyword research, optimize your video titles, descriptions, and tags, and create engaging thumbnails to attract more viewers.

Share on Social Media: Leverage your social media presence to promote your viral content. Share snippets or teasers of your video on platforms like Instagram, Twitter, and Facebook, and encourage your followers to watch the full video on YouTube. Engage with your audience, respond to comments, and encourage them to share your content with their networks.

Collaborate with Influencers: Collaborating with influencers or other creators in your niche can significantly expand your reach. By collaborating on a video or featuring each other's content, you can tap into their audience and leverage their influence to promote your viral content.

Engage with Your Audience: Actively engaging with your audience is crucial for promoting viral content. Respond to comments, encourage viewers to like, share, and subscribe, and create a sense of community around your content. This not only boosts engagement but also encourages viewers to become advocates for your content and share it with their networks.

In this chapter, we explored the power of trending topics and viral content on YouTube. We discussed strategies for identifying trending topics, creating viral content, and promoting it effectively. By understanding the dynamics of trending topics and leveraging their potential, you can attract a wider audience, increase engagement, and ultimately enhance your chances of making millions from YouTube.

Remember, while viral success cannot be guaranteed, combining creativity, strategic thinking, and an understanding of your audience's preferences can significantly increase your chances of creating content that captivates the world. Embrace the power of trends and set your channel on the path to viral success.

Part IV

Advanced Strategies for Success

Chapter 22

Developing a Content Strategy

By reaching this chapter, you've already taken significant steps towards making millions from YouTube. Now, it's time to delve into the crucial aspect of developing a compelling content strategy. In this chapter, we'll explore the key elements you need to consider to create engaging content that will attract and retain a loyal audience. Remember, a well-crafted content strategy can be the driving force behind your success on YouTube. So, let's get started!

Before you can create content that resonates with your viewers, it's essential to understand who your target audience is. Engage with your audience through comments, social media, and surveys to gain valuable insights into what they want to see from you. By knowing your audience inside out, you can create content that not only captures their attention but also compels them to keep coming back for more

Identifying Your Unique Value Proposition:

With millions of YouTube channels out there, it's crucial to identify what sets you apart from the competition. What unique value can you provide to your viewers? Take some time to reflect on your skills, expertise, and passions. Consider your personal story and what makes you authentic. Use these insights to define your unique value proposition, which will form the foundation of your content strategy. Make sure to communicate this value clearly to your audience, so they understand why they should choose your channel over others.

Defining Your Content Pillars:

Content pillars are the main topics or themes that will be the focus of your channel. They should align with your unique value proposition and resonate with your target audience. Brainstorm ideas and create a list of potential content pillars. These can be broad topics or niches that allow you to explore different angles within each one. For example, if you're a fitness enthusiast, your content pillars could include workout routines, nutrition tips, and mental well-being. Having well-defined content pillars will not only give your channel a clear identity but also help you stay consistent and focused in your content creation.

Crafting Engaging Video Formats:

Now that you have your content pillars, it's time to think about the various video formats you can use to deliver your content effectively. Experiment with different formats such as tutorials, vlogs, interviews, challenges, or storytelling. Each format offers a unique way to engage with your audience and keeps your content fresh and exciting. Remember, variety is the spice of life, so don't be afraid to mix it up and surprise your viewers with new and captivating video formats.

Planning Your Content Calendar:

Consistency is key on YouTube. Developing a content calendar will help you stay organized and ensure you consistently deliver content to your audience. Start by outlining your content pillars and assign specific topics or ideas to each week or month. A content calendar will also help you plan for seasonal or trending topics and allow you to collaborate with other creators for cross-promotion opportunities. Additionally, schedule regular time for brainstorming new ideas and assessing the performance of your existing content.

Optimizing SEO for Discoverability:

Implementing Search Engine Optimization (SEO) strategies can significantly enhance your visibility on YouTube. Conduct keyword research using tools like Google Trends, YouTube's autocomplete feature, or dedicated SEO software. Incorporate relevant keywords in your video titles, descriptions, tags, and captions. This will increase the chances of your content appearing in search results and recommendations, ultimately driving more traffic to your channel.

Building a loyal community is a vital aspect of a successful YouTube channel. Actively engage with your audience by responding to comments, asking for their input, and creating opportunities for interaction. Encourage viewers to like, share, and subscribe to your channel, and reward them for their support. Host live streams, Q&A sessions, or contests to foster a sense of belonging and make your viewers feel appreciated. Remember, your audience is your biggest asset, so make them an integral part of your content strategy.

Analysing and Iterating:

To continuously improve your content strategy, it's crucial to analyze the performance of your videos and make data-driven decisions. Utilize YouTube Analytics to gain insights into your viewership, engagement, and audience retention. Identify trends, patterns, and areas for improvement. Pay attention to which videos perform exceptionally well and try to replicate their success. Similarly, assess the videos that underperform and identify the reasons behind their lack of engagement. You can improve your content strategy over time and assure the expansion and success of your channel by analysing and iterating.

Developing a content strategy is a critical step on your journey to making millions from YouTube. By understanding your target audience, defining your unique value proposition, and crafting engaging video formats, you can create content that captivates viewers and keeps them coming back for more. To improve strengthen your plan, create a content calendar, boost SEO, interact with your audience, and track your results. Remember, building a successful YouTube channel takes time, effort, and dedication, but with a compelling content strategy, you'll be well on your way to achieving your goals. Now, go out there and create content that makes a lasting impact!

Chapter 23

Expanding Your YouTube Presence

By reaching this chapter, you've already made significant progress on your journey to YouTube success. Now, it's time to explore strategies that will help you expand your YouTube presence and reach a wider audience. In this chapter, we will dive deep into unique and effective techniques that will set you apart from the competition and propel your channel to new heights. Get ready to unleash your creativity, engage with your audience, and take your YouTube presence to the next level!

Develop a Multi-Platform Strategy:

Expanding your YouTube presence involves more than just creating videos. It's about building a brand and reaching your audience across multiple platforms. Consider leveraging other social media platforms, such as Instagram, Twitter, and TikTok, to amplify your content and engage with a broader audience. Tailor your content for each platform while maintaining a cohesive brand identity. Use Instagram to share behind-the-scenes glimpses, Twitter for engaging in conversations, and TikTok for creating short, captivating teasers. By diversifying your presence, you'll increase your chances of attracting new viewers and driving traffic to your YouTube channel.

Harness the Power of Influencer Marketing:

Influencer marketing is a game-changer when it comes to expanding your YouTube presence. Identify influencers in your niche or related fields who have a substantial following and align with your brand values. Collaborate with them to create sponsored content or product endorsements that introduce your channel to their audience. This strategy can provide an instant boost in visibility and attract new viewers who are more likely to subscribe and engage with your content. Remember to choose influencers whose audience aligns with your target demographic for the best results.

Optimize Your Video Distribution Strategy:

Expanding your YouTube presence requires getting your videos in front of as many eyes as possible. To achieve this, optimize your video distribution strategy. Consider repurposing your content for other platforms, such as Facebook or LinkedIn, to reach new audiences. Create teaser clips or highlights of your YouTube videos to share on these platforms, with a clear call-to-action to watch the full video on your channel. Additionally, explore partnerships with media outlets or websites that are relevant to your content. By distributing your videos strategically, you'll expand your reach and attract viewers who may not have discovered your channel otherwise.

Create Compelling and Shareable Content:

To expand your YouTube presence, it's crucial to create content that captivates viewers and inspires them to share it with others. Focus on crafting high-quality videos that provide value, entertainment, or education. Consider incorporating storytelling techniques, humor, or emotional elements to create an emotional connection with your audience. Engage your viewers by asking questions, encouraging comments, and initiating discussions. The more shareable and engaging your content is, the more likely it will be shared across social media platforms, leading to increased visibility and new viewership for your channel.

Host Collaborative Projects and Challenges:

Collaborative projects and challenges are excellent opportunities to expand your YouTube presence. Collaborate with other creators to work on joint projects or challenges that cater to both of your audiences. This cross-promotion allows you to tap into new viewers who may be interested in your content but haven't discovered your channel yet. Choose collaborators who share a similar target audience but bring a fresh perspective or expertise to the table. By creating collaborative projects, you not only expand your reach but also build relationships within the YouTube community, opening doors to future opportunities.

Engage in Thought Leadership:

Establishing yourself as a thought leader in your niche can significantly expand your YouTube presence. Share your expertise, insights, and unique perspectives through educational or informative videos. Provide value by addressing common challenges, answering frequently asked questions, or sharing industry trends and predictions. By positioning yourself as an authority, viewers will trust your content and be more likely to subscribe and share it with others. Engage with your audience in the comments section, respond to their questions, and seek feedback. Thought leadership not only expands your reach but also builds credibility and fosters a loyal community.

Leverage YouTube Live and Premieres:

YouTube offers powerful features like live streaming and premieres that can help you expand your presence and engage with your audience in real-time. Plan and promote live streams or premieres to build anticipation and excitement. Use this opportunity to interact with your viewers, answer their questions, and give them a behind-the-scenes look at your content creation process. Live streams and premieres foster a sense of exclusivity and urgency, encouraging viewers to join in and become active participants in your channel. By leveraging these features, you'll attract new viewers and strengthen the bond with your existing audience.

Collaborate with Brands:

Expanding your YouTube presence can also involve collaborating with brands. As your channel grows, brands may approach you for sponsored content or product integrations. Select brand partnerships that align with your channel's values and resonate with your audience. Ensure that any sponsored content feels authentic and adds value to your viewers' experience. Collaborating with brands not only provides financial opportunities but also exposes your channel to a wider audience through brand promotions and endorsements.

Expanding your YouTube presence requires a combination of creativity, strategic thinking, and active engagement with your audience. Develop a multi-platform strategy, harness the power of influencer marketing, optimize your video distribution strategy, create compelling and shareable content, host collaborative projects and challenges, engage in thought leadership, leverage YouTube Live and Premieres, and collaborate with brands. Embrace experimentation, stay true to your brand, and consistently deliver high-quality content.

Remember, expanding your YouTube presence is a journey that requires dedication, adaptability, and a deep understanding of your audience. With the right strategies and a passion for creating exceptional content, you can take your YouTube presence to new heights and unlock the potential for making millions from YouTube. Keep pushing boundaries, be open to learning, and watch your channel flourish in the vast YouTube landscape. The possibilities are limitless!

Chapter 24

Internationalizing Your Channel

Congratulations! By reaching this chapter, it's evident that your YouTube channel is flourishing. You have built a strong presence, gained a significant following, and are now ready to take your content to a global level. In this chapter, we will explore the exciting opportunities and strategies for internationalizing your channel, allowing you to expand your reach, engage with diverse audiences, and potentially multiply your success.

The Power of Going Global

Taking your channel international opens up a world of possibilities. With over 2 billion monthly active users on YouTube and an increasingly interconnected world, there's a vast audience waiting to discover your content. Internationalizing your channel can lead to exponential growth, brand expansion, and lucrative partnerships.

Research Your Target Markets

Before diving into international waters, it's crucial to conduct thorough research on potential target markets. Explore regions, countries, and demographics where your content is likely to resonate. Consider factors such as language, culture, interests, and existing competition. Identifying target markets will help you tailor your content and marketing strategies accordingly.

Localization is Key

To successfully connect with international audiences, localization is essential. Localization involves adapting your content to suit the preferences, language, and cultural nuances of your target market. This includes translating video titles, descriptions, and subtitles, as well as considering regional trends, humor, and references. Hiring professional translators and cultural consultants can greatly assist in maintaining authenticity and relatability.

Collaborate with Local Creators

Collaborating with local creators from your target markets can be a powerful way to expand your reach and establish credibility. Seek out popular creators who align with your content and have a strong presence in your desired regions. Joint projects, guest appearances, and cross-promotion can help you tap into their existing audience and gain valuable exposure.

Understand Regional SEO

Understanding regional SEO is crucial when targeting international audiences on YouTube. Search Engine Optimization plays a significant role in improving the discoverability of your content, and it becomes even more important when trying to reach viewers in specific regions. Here are some additional details to help you grasp the concept and implement effective regional SEO strategies:

Research Local Keywords: Conduct thorough keyword research in the target market's language. Identify the terms and phrases that local viewers are likely to use when searching for content similar to yours. Tools like Google Keyword Planner, SEMrush, or Ahrefs can assist you in finding popular keywords in specific regions. Incorporate these keywords naturally into your video titles, descriptions, and tags.

Optimize Video Titles and Descriptions: Craft compelling and descriptive video titles that incorporate relevant keywords for the target market. Ensure that the titles accurately reflect the content of your videos and entice viewers to click. Similarly, optimize your video descriptions by including keywords and providing a comprehensive summary of your video. This helps YouTube's algorithm understand the content of your videos and improve their visibility in search results.

Utilize Localized Tags: Tags are an essential part of YouTube's search algorithm. Include region-specific tags that relate to your content and align with the interests and preferences of the target audience. Use a mix of general and specific tags to cover a broad range of search queries. Regularly review and update your tags based on keyword performance and trending topics in each region.

Translate and Localize: When optimizing your content for international audiences, it's crucial to translate your titles, descriptions, and tags accurately. Avoid using automated translation tools as they may not capture the nuances and cultural context effectively. Hire professional translators who are fluent in the target language to ensure accurate localization. Localized content demonstrates your commitment to connecting with the local audience and improves the chances of appearing in relevant search results.

Leverage Regional Trends and Topics: Stay informed about regional trends, events, and popular topics in your target markets. Incorporate these trends into your content, titles, descriptions, and tags to increase the relevance of your videos. By aligning your content with what's currently popular in the region, you increase the likelihood of appearing in searches and attracting viewers who are interested in those topics.

Analyze and Optimize: Regularly analyze the performance of your videos in each target market. Pay attention to metrics such as views, watch time, engagement, and audience retention. YouTube's analytics tools provide valuable insights into audience behavior, allowing you to identify what works and what doesn't. Based on this data, make adjustments to your SEO strategy, including refining keywords, updating titles, and optimizing descriptions to improve the visibility and performance of your videos.

Remember, SEO is an ongoing process. Stay updated with the latest SEO best practices and algorithm changes on YouTube to ensure that your content remains optimized for discoverability. By understanding regional SEO and implementing effective strategies, you can increase your chances of reaching the right viewers in different international markets and grow your YouTube channel's global presence.

Tailor Content to Local Preferences

While your core content may remain consistent, tailoring it to suit local preferences can significantly enhance engagement. Study the content landscape in your target markets to understand what resonates with viewers. Incorporate local trends, topics, and storytelling styles while staying true to your unique voice. Flexibility and adaptability are key to maintaining relevance across borders.

Embrace Cultural Sensitivity

Cultural sensitivity is vital when creating content for diverse audiences. Be aware of cultural taboos, traditions, and sensitivities in each target market to avoid inadvertently offending or alienating viewers. Demonstrating respect and understanding through your content will foster trust and connection, encouraging viewers to engage with your channel.

Optimize Timing and Scheduling

Different time zones can pose a challenge when targeting international viewers. Experiment with scheduling your uploads to align with peak viewing times in your target markets. Consider using YouTube's analytics tools to identify when your international audience is most active and adjust your publishing schedule accordingly. Consistency and regularity will help build an international audience base.

Leverage Social Media Platforms

Expand your reach beyond YouTube by utilizing popular social media platforms in your target markets. Each region has its preferred platforms, such as Weibo in China or VKontakte in Russia. Create accounts and share snippets of your content, teasers, behind-the-scenes footage, and engage with the local audience. Linking your social media profiles to your YouTube channel will drive traffic and foster cross-platform growth.

Engage with Your International Audience

Building a strong community is vital for any successful YouTube channel. Make an effort to interact with your international audience by responding to comments, hosting live streams, and conducting Q&A sessions. Encourage viewers to share their thoughts, suggestions, and even collaborate with you. Engaging with your audience fosters loyalty, deepens connections, and fuels international growth.

Monitor Analytics and Adapt

As you embark on your internationalization journey, regularly monitor your analytics to gain insights into audience demographics, viewing patterns, and engagement metrics. YouTube's analytics tools provide valuable data that can guide your content strategy and help you make informed decisions. Adapt your approach based on the feedback received, optimizing for growth and success in each target market.

Internationalizing your YouTube channel presents a world of opportunities. By conducting thorough research, localizing your content, collaborating with local creators, and understanding regional preferences, you can tap into new markets and expand your reach globally. Remember to embrace cultural sensitivity, optimize timing, leverage social media platforms, engage with your international audience, and adapt based on analytics. With dedication, creativity, and a global mindset, you can make your mark on the international YouTube scene and continue to make millions.

Go forth, explore the world, and create content that resonates with audiences across borders. The sky's the limit for your international YouTube success!

Remember, the world is waiting to discover your talent. Start your internationalization journey today!

Chapter 25

Scaling Your Channel with a Team

CONGRATULATIONS ON YOUR JOURNEY to becoming a successful YouTuber! By this point, you have likely realized the immense potential that YouTube offers for making millions. However, as your channel grows and evolves, you may find it challenging to handle all the demands on your own. That's where scaling your channel with a team becomes crucial. In this chapter, we will delve into the benefits of building a team, the various roles you can consider, and effective strategies for managing and growing your YouTube empire.

The Power of a Team

Building a team for your YouTube channel can be a game-changer in terms of productivity, creativity, and overall growth. Here are some key advantages of scaling your channel with a team:

Enhanced Content Creation: A team brings together a diverse range of skills, expertise, and perspectives. Collaborating with others allows you to produce content that is more engaging, diverse, and appealing to a broader audience. By leveraging the strengths of each team member, you can create high-quality videos that captivate viewers and keep them coming back for more.

Increased Efficiency: As your channel expands, the workload can become overwhelming. By delegating tasks to team members, you can lighten your own load and focus on strategic decisions and high-level content creation. Sharing responsibilities allows you to accomplish more in less time, ensuring a consistent output of top-notch videos.

Expanded Reach: Each team member can contribute to promoting your channel, engaging with the audience, and reaching out to potential collaborators or sponsors. With a team effort, your channel can gain more exposure and grow faster. By leveraging the networks and connections of your team members, you can tap into new audiences and expand your reach beyond what you could achieve alone.

Continuous Growth: Building a team brings fresh ideas, insights, and creativity to your channel. As your team members contribute their unique perspectives, you can experiment with different content formats, explore innovative strategies, and tackle new opportunities. This collaborative approach ensures that your channel remains dynamic and continues to evolve, attracting new viewers and keeping your existing audience engaged.

Roles to Consider

To effectively scale your channel with a team, it's crucial to identify the roles and responsibilities that need to be filled. Here are some key roles commonly found in successful YouTube teams:

Content Creators: These individuals are responsible for producing videos and maintaining the creative quality of your channel. They may specialize in various content formats, such as vlogs, tutorials, reviews, or entertainment. Content creators bring their unique personalities, talents, and expertise to the table, ensuring a diverse range of content that appeals to different segments of your audience.

Editors: Editors play a critical role in refining and enhancing your videos. They handle tasks like video editing, color correction, sound mixing, and adding visual effects. Skilled editors can elevate the production value of your content, create a consistent brand aesthetic, and ensure that each video is polished and professional.

Social Media Managers: Social media managers are responsible for maintaining an active presence on platforms like Instagram, Twitter, and Facebook. They engage with your audience, promote your videos, and create buzz around your channel. Social media managers also handle community management, responding to comments and messages, and fostering a sense of connection and loyalty among your followers.

SEO Specialists: Search Engine Optimization (SEO) specialists focus on optimizing your videos and channel for search engines. They conduct keyword research, write compelling titles and descriptions, and implement strategies to improve your channel's visibility in search results. SEO specialists ensure that your content is discoverable, helping you reach a wider audience and increase your channel's organic growth.

Graphic Designers: Graphic designers play a crucial role in creating visually appealing thumbnails, channel banners, and other visual assets. They help your videos stand out in crowded search results and convey your brand identity effectively. With their expertise in design and aesthetics, graphic designers ensure that your channel has a cohesive and visually appealing presence.

Business Managers: As your channel grows, it's essential to have someone who can handle the business side of things. Business managers take care of partnerships, sponsorships, monetization, and negotiations. They have a keen eye for identifying revenue opportunities, building relationships with brands, and maximizing your channel's earning potential. Business managers allow you to focus on content creation while ensuring that your channel remains profitable and sustainable.

Managing Your YouTube Empire

Once you have a team in place, effective management becomes crucial to ensure smooth collaboration and maximize your team's potential. Here are some tips for managing your YouTube empire:

Clear Communication: Establish open and transparent communication channels with your team members. Regularly communicate your vision, goals, and expectations. Encourage feedback, brainstorming, and collaboration. Use tools like project management software or messaging apps to facilitate communication and keep everyone on the same page.

Delegation and Empowerment: Delegate tasks based on individual strengths and expertise. Empower your team members to take ownership of their responsibilities and make decisions. Trust their abilities and provide them with the necessary resources and support to excel. By empowering your team members, you create a sense of ownership and foster a culture of innovation and initiative.

Continuous Learning and Development: Encourage your team members to stay updated with industry trends, best practices, and emerging technologies. Invest in their professional development through training, workshops, and conferences. By providing opportunities for growth and learning, you not only enhance their skills but also foster a sense of loyalty and commitment among your team members.

Performance Evaluation and Feedback: Regularly evaluate your team's performance and provide constructive feedback. Recognize and reward their achievements, both individually and as a team. Address any issues or challenges promptly and offer guidance for improvement. By providing a supportive and constructive environment, you encourage your team members to continuously strive for excellence.

Flexibility and Adaptability: Understand that team dynamics and individual circumstances can change over time. Be flexible and adaptable in accommodating the evolving needs and aspirations of your team members. Foster a healthy work-life balance and consider flexible working arrangements if feasible. By prioritizing the well-being and growth of your team members, you create a positive and productive work environment.

Team Building and Bonding: Organize team-building activities, social events, or retreats to strengthen the bond among your team members. Foster a positive and collaborative work culture where everyone feels valued and motivated. By fostering a sense of camaraderie and teamwork, you create an environment that encourages creativity, innovation, and a shared commitment to your channel's success.

Growing Your YouTube Empire

As your channel continues to grow, you may need to expand your team further or explore new opportunities. Here are some strategies to consider:

Specialization: Identify areas where your channel can benefit from specialized roles. For example, you may hire a dedicated scriptwriter, animation expert, or data analyst to enhance your content and channel performance. By bringing in specialists, you can further elevate the quality and impact of your videos.

Collaboration and Cross-Promotion: Collaborate with other YouTubers or influencers in your niche to tap into their audience and expand your reach. Cross-promotion allows you to introduce your channel to new viewers and create mutually beneficial partnerships. By leveraging the influence and reach of others, you can exponentially grow your subscriber base.

Strategic Partnerships: Seek strategic partnerships with brands, media companies, or production studios. Such collaborations can provide additional resources, exposure, and opportunities for your channel. Strategic partnerships can open doors to new revenue streams, sponsorship deals, and production support, allowing you to take your channel to new heights.

Monetization Beyond YouTube: Explore diversifying your revenue streams by venturing into merchandising, brand sponsorships, affiliate marketing, or creating premium content for subscription-based platforms. By expanding your monetization strategies beyond YouTube's ad revenue, you can maximize your earnings and build a more sustainable business model.

International Expansion: Consider reaching out to international audiences by translating or localizing your content. Hire translators or subtitle specialists to make your videos accessible to non-native speakers. By tapping into global markets, you can broaden your reach and attract a diverse audience base.

Scaling your channel with a team is a pivotal step in taking your YouTube empire to new heights. By leveraging the power of teamwork, you can enhance content creation, increase efficiency, expand your reach, and foster continuous growth. Carefully consider the roles and responsibilities that need to be filled, and build a team of talented individuals who share your passion and vision.

With effective management, clear communication, and a collaborative spirit, your team can work together seamlessly to create exceptional content and drive the success of your channel. As you continue to grow, explore new opportunities, and diversify your revenue streams, your YouTube empire has the potential to make millions and offer a fulfilling and rewarding journey as a content creator.

Chapter 26

Creating Evergreen Content

IN THE EVER-EVOLVING WORLD of YouTube, where trends come and go in the blink of an eye, creating content that stands the test of time is no easy feat. However, if you can crack the code to producing evergreen content, you'll unlock a powerful strategy that can help you make millions from YouTube. In this chapter, we'll delve into the secrets of creating timeless videos that continue to attract viewers long after their initial upload.

What is Evergreen Content?

Videos that your audience finds helpful and relevant over an extended period of time are referred to as evergreen content. Unlike trendy or time-sensitive content, which loses its relevance quickly, evergreen content continues to attract views, engagement, and monetization opportunities long after its initial release. By focusing on creating evergreen content, you can build a sustainable YouTube channel with a steady stream of views and income.

Benefits of Evergreen Content

Longevity: Evergreen content has the advantage of remaining relevant and valuable to your audience over an extended period. Unlike trendy or time-sensitive content, which loses its relevance quickly, evergreen videos continue to attract views and engagement long after their initial release. This ensures a steady flow of traffic to your channel and a sustained impact on your audience.

Increased Searchability: Evergreen content is highly searchable. By creating videos that provide valuable information, answer common questions, or offer practical solutions, you increase the chances of your content appearing in search results. This leads to a consistent influx of new viewers discovering your channel and can significantly enhance your channel's visibility and reach.

Consistent Traffic: Due to their lasting relevance, evergreen videos attract a consistent flow of traffic to your channel. While trendy videos may experience a surge of views and engagement for a short period, evergreen content continues to attract viewers over months or even years. This consistent traffic helps to build a stable and sustainable viewership base for your channel.

Authority Building: Evergreen content allows you to establish yourself as an authority in your niche. By consistently producing high-quality videos that offer valuable insights or expert advice, you position yourself as a reliable source of information. Over time, this authority can lead to increased opportunities for collaborations, sponsorships, and other partnerships.

Monetization Opportunities: Evergreen content opens up multiple monetization avenues. With a steady stream of views and engagement, you can generate revenue through ads, sponsorships, affiliate marketing, and even selling your own products or services. The longevity of evergreen content ensures that these monetization opportunities can be sustained over time, providing a reliable income stream from your YouTube channel.

Enhanced Brand Image: Creating evergreen content demonstrates a commitment to quality and valuable content. By consistently producing videos that stand the test of time, you build a positive brand image and reputation. This helps to attract and retain loyal viewers who appreciate the value you provide, leading to increased engagement, shares, and positive word-of-mouth.

Versatility and Repurposing: Evergreen content has the advantage of versatility. You can repurpose your evergreen videos into different formats, such as blog posts, podcasts, or infographics. This allows you to reach a wider audience across various platforms and extend the lifespan of your content. Repurposing also provides opportunities for cross-promotion and collaboration with other content creators.

Increased Subscriber Base: Evergreen content attracts viewers who are genuinely interested in the topics you cover. By consistently delivering valuable and relevant content, you increase the likelihood of viewers subscribing to your channel. As your subscriber base grows, you gain a loyal audience that is more likely to engage with your future content, share it with others, and contribute to the growth of your channel.

Educational Value: Evergreen content often focuses on providing educational value to viewers. By creating videos that teach new skills, explain complex concepts, or offer practical tips, you become a valuable resource for your audience. This educational value fosters a sense of loyalty and appreciation, as viewers recognize the benefit they gain from your content.

Sustainability: Evergreen content provides a sustainable foundation for your YouTube channel. While it's essential to stay updated with current trends and adapt to the changing landscape of YouTube, having a library of evergreen videos ensures that you always have a reliable source of views and engagement. This sustainability contributes to the long-term success and growth of your channel, allowing you to make millions from YouTube.

Tips for Creating Evergreen Content

Focus on Timeless Topics: When brainstorming video ideas, prioritize topics that have longevity. Look for subjects that have a broad appeal and are unlikely to become outdated quickly. For example, tutorials, educational content, and "how-to" guides tend to be evergreen because people will always be searching for information and learning new skills.

Solve Problems: Identify common pain points or problems faced by your target audience and create videos that provide practical solutions. By offering valuable solutions, you position yourself as a go-to resource for your viewers, ensuring the long-term relevance of your content.

Conduct keyword research: Do extensive keyword research to find the most used search terms and phrases in your niche. Incorporate these keywords strategically into your video titles, descriptions, and tags to improve your chances of appearing in search results and attracting organic traffic.

Quality Production: Invest in high-quality production to make your videos visually appealing and professional. While trends in editing styles may come and go, ensuring that your content is visually polished and well-produced will help it stand the test of time.

Create Evergreen Series: Develop a series of videos around a specific theme or topic. By creating a cohesive series, you can provide a consistent flow of evergreen content that keeps viewers coming back for more. Additionally, organizing your content into playlists makes it easier for viewers to navigate and discover related videos on your channel.

Repurpose Content: Consider repurposing your evergreen content into different formats. By repackaging your content in various formats, you can reach a wider audience and extend the lifespan of your evergreen material.

Keep Updating: Even evergreen content can benefit from occasional updates. As technology advances or new information becomes available, revisit your existing videos and make necessary revisions or additions. This ensures that your content remains accurate and up to date, enhancing its value to viewers.

Creating evergreen content is an essential strategy for building a successful YouTube channel and making millions. By focusing on timeless topics, providing valuable solutions, and optimizing your content for searchability, you can attract a steady stream of viewers and open up various monetization opportunities. Remember, the key to evergreen content is to provide lasting value to your audience and position yourself as an authority in your niche. With dedication, creativity, and a commitment to quality, you can create videos that continue to reap rewards long after their initial release.

Chapter 27

Building Your Personal Brand

IN TODAY'S DIGITAL LANDSCAPE, YouTube has become a platform where ordinary individuals can turn their passion into a lucrative business opportunity. With millions of users and billions of hours of content consumed daily, YouTube offers tremendous potential for individuals to make millions. However, amidst the sea of creators, it is crucial to establish a strong personal brand that sets you apart from the competition. In this chapter, we will explore the strategies and techniques to build and cultivate a powerful personal brand on YouTube, setting you on the path to success and financial abundance.

Unleash Your Authenticity:

At the core of a successful personal brand lies authenticity. In a world full of copycats and imitators, embracing your unique voice and perspective will enable you to connect with your audience on a deeper level. Authenticity is the key to building trust, and trust is the foundation upon which your brand will flourish. Share your stories, passions, and quirks with your viewers. Let them see the real you and form a genuine connection that will keep them coming back for more.

Define Your Niche:

To stand out in the vast YouTube ecosystem, it is essential to define your niche. Identify your areas of expertise, interests, and the audience you want to cater to. Find a balance between your passion and what the market demands. By niching down, you position yourself as an authority in your chosen field, making it easier for viewers to associate your personal brand with a specific subject matter. This focused approach will attract a dedicated audience who are more likely to engage with your content and become loyal followers.

Craft Your Unique Selling Proposition (USP):

What makes you unique? What sets you apart from the thousands of other creators vying for attention? Your unique selling proposition (USP) is the differentiating factor that defines your personal brand. It could be your storytelling skills, expertise, humor, or innovative approach. Identify your USP and consistently leverage it across your content. This will help viewers understand why they should choose your channel over others and create a memorable impression that reinforces your brand.

Develop a Compelling Brand Identity:

A cohesive and visually appealing brand identity is crucial for capturing and retaining viewer attention. Invest time and effort in creating a consistent brand identity that resonates with your target audience. Consider elements such as your channel name, logo, color palette, typography, and visual style. These components should reflect your personality, niche, and the emotions you want your brand to evoke. Consistency in your branding will make it easier for viewers to recognize and remember your channel.

Collaborate with Like-Minded Creators:

Collaborating with other creators can be a powerful way to expand your reach and tap into new audiences. Seek out like-minded creators within your niche and explore collaboration opportunities. Collaborative videos allow you to cross-pollinate your audiences, introduce yourself to new viewers, and gain exposure in the process. When choosing collaborators, ensure their values align with yours, and their content complements yours. Successful collaborations can provide a win-win situation, helping both parties grow their personal brands.

Consistency in Content Creation:

Consistency is key when it comes to building your personal brand on YouTube. Establishing a regular upload schedule not only helps viewers know when to expect new content but also signals your commitment and professionalism. Stick to your schedule as much as possible, but also prioritize quality over quantity. Delivering valuable and well-produced content consistently will keep your audience engaged and coming back for more.

Optimize Your Video Titles, Descriptions, and Tags:

To attract viewers and improve discoverability, optimize your video titles, descriptions, and tags with relevant keywords. Conduct thorough keyword research to understand what terms your target audience is searching for. Craft compelling titles that pique curiosity and accurately represent your content. Write informative and engaging descriptions that provide additional context and encourage viewers to watch. Lastly, tag your videos strategically with relevant keywords to increase your chances of appearing in search results and suggested videos.

Leverage Social Media Platforms:

While YouTube is the cornerstone of your personal brand, leveraging social media platforms can amplify your reach and engagement. Create accounts on platforms such as Instagram, Twitter, Facebook, and TikTok to extend your brand's presence beyond YouTube. Tailor your content to each platform's unique format and engage with your audience through posts, stories, and live videos. Social media allows you to share behind-the-scenes glimpses, tease upcoming content, and build a closer connection with your followers.

Seek Sponsorship and Monetization Opportunities:

As your personal brand grows, you'll have opportunities to monetize your YouTube channel through sponsorships, brand partnerships, and advertising. When seeking sponsorships, prioritize alignment with your brand values and audience interests. Choose partners whose products or services genuinely benefit your viewers. The trust you've built with your audience should always come first. Additionally, explore other revenue streams such as merchandise sales, affiliate marketing, and direct fan support platforms like Patreon.

Continuously Evolve and Adapt:

The digital landscape is ever-changing, and what works today may not work tomorrow. Stay abreast of industry trends, platform updates, and shifts in viewer preferences. Adapt your content strategy, formats, and presentation style to remain relevant and appealing to your audience. Embrace experimentation, analyze viewer feedback and engagement metrics, and be willing to evolve your personal brand to stay ahead of the curve.

Building a personal brand is not a one-way street. Interaction and engagement with your audience are vital for fostering a loyal community. Respond to comments, ask questions, and encourage discussion. Show genuine interest in your viewers' opinions and make them feel heard. Additionally, leverage community features like polls, Q&A sessions, and live streams to provide valuable, interactive experiences that deepen the connection between you and your audience.

Building a personal brand on YouTube is an exciting and rewarding journey. By embracing authenticity, defining your niche, crafting a compelling brand identity, engaging with your audience, collaborating with others, staying consistent, optimizing your content, leveraging social media, seeking sponsorship opportunities, and continuously evolving, you can pave the way to making millions from YouTube. Remember, building a personal brand takes time and dedication, but with passion and perseverance, your YouTube channel can become a thriving business venture that generates not just millions, but also lasting impact and fulfillment.

Part V

Managing and Leveraging Success

Chapter 28

Time Management and Productivity Tips

In the world of YouTube, time is a valuable asset. As a content creator, you have to juggle numerous tasks such as brainstorming ideas, filming, editing, promoting, and engaging with your audience. It's easy to get overwhelmed and lose track of time, but with effective time management and productivity techniques, you can maximize your efficiency and propel your channel to success. In this chapter, we will explore a variety of tips and strategies to help you make the most of your time and achieve your goals on YouTube.

Set Clear Goals and Prioritize Tasks

Before diving into your daily routine, it's crucial to establish clear goals for your YouTube channel. What do you want to achieve? How many videos do you plan to publish each week? How many subscribers or views do you aim to reach?

Use tools like to-do lists, project management software, or productivity apps to organize your tasks and keep track of deadlines. By focusing on the most critical tasks first, you'll ensure that you are always working towards your long-term goals.

Plan and Schedule Your Time

Creating a schedule is essential for effective time management. Allocate specific time blocks for different activities such as brainstorming, filming, editing, and promoting your videos. When making a schedule, take into account your energy levels and production trends. Some people are more productive in the morning, while others thrive in the late hours. Tailor your schedule to align with your personal preferences and maximize your efficiency.

Avoid overcommitting yourself and be realistic about the time required for each task. Leave some buffer time for unexpected events or delays. Additionally, make sure to schedule breaks to rest and recharge. Working non-stop can lead to burnout and decreased productivity in the long run.

Eliminate Time-Wasting Activities

One of the biggest challenges in time management is overcoming distractions and avoiding time-wasting activities. Identify the activities that eat up your time without adding value to your YouTube channel. Common culprits include excessive social media scrolling, watching unrelated YouTube videos, or getting caught up in unproductive discussions.

To combat these distractions, consider using time management techniques such as the Pomodoro Technique. Set a timer for a specific period, like 25 minutes, and work on a task with full focus. After the timer goes off, take a short break before diving back into another focused work session. This technique helps you maintain concentration and prevents burnout.

Delegate and Outsource

As your YouTube channel grows, it may become challenging to handle every aspect of content creation on your own. Consider delegating tasks or outsourcing certain responsibilities to others. For example, you can hire a video editor, a social media manager, or a virtual assistant to handle administrative tasks. This allows you to focus on creating high-quality content and building relationships with your audience.

Delegating also applies to your personal life. If you find yourself spending a significant amount of time on household chores or other non-essential activities, consider hiring help or involving family members to share the responsibilities. By freeing up your time, you can dedicate more energy to your YouTube endeavors.

Automate and Streamline Processes

Take advantage of technology and automation tools to streamline your workflows and save time. Look for opportunities to automate repetitive tasks such as video uploads, social media posts, or email responses. Use scheduling tools to plan your content releases in advance, allowing you to maintain a consistent posting schedule without constant manual effort.

Explore video editing software that offers templates, presets, or shortcuts to speed up your editing process. Invest in tools that help with keyword research, audience analytics, or SEO optimization to improve the discoverability and performance of your videos. By automating and streamlining processes, you can allocate more time to creative and strategic aspects of your YouTube channel.

Optimize Your Workflow

Efficiency in your workflow is key to maximizing productivity. Identify any bottlenecks or areas where you frequently encounter obstacles. Look for ways to eliminate or mitigate these challenges. For example, if video rendering takes a long time, optimize your computer's performance or consider upgrading your equipment.

Create templates or standardized processes for repetitive tasks to minimize decision-making and streamline your workflow. Develop a consistent folder structure for your files, use naming conventions, and establish a logical organization system to easily locate and access your assets. These small adjustments can save you valuable time in the long run.

Focus on Deep Work

In the age of constant notifications and distractions, finding time for deep, focused work is crucial. Deep work refers to uninterrupted, concentrated periods of time where you can tackle complex tasks and produce high-quality work. This can include tasks such as scripting, researching, or editing videos.

To create a conducive environment for deep work, eliminate distractions by turning off notifications, finding a quiet space, or using productivity apps that block access to distracting websites or apps during designated work periods. Set specific blocks of time solely dedicated to deep work and communicate your availability to minimize interruptions.

Take Care of Your Well-being

Productivity is not just about managing your time; it's also about taking care of yourself. Prioritize your physical and mental well-being to maintain high levels of productivity in the long term. Get enough sleep, eat a balanced diet, and engage in regular exercise to keep your body and mind in optimal condition.

Incorporate stress-management techniques such as meditation, deep breathing exercises, or regular breaks to prevent burnout and maintain focus. Establish a healthy work-life balance by setting boundaries and scheduling time for leisure, hobbies, and spending quality time with loved ones. Taking care of yourself will enhance your creativity, energy levels, and overall productivity.

Time management and productivity are essential skills for YouTube content creators. By implementing these strategies and tips, you can make the most of your time, increase your efficiency, and propel your YouTube channel to new heights. Remember to set clear goals, plan your time effectively, eliminate time-wasting activities, delegate and outsource when necessary, automate and streamline processes, optimize your workflow, focus on deep work, and prioritize your well-being. With discipline, focus, and smart time management, you'll be well on your way to making millions from YouTube.

Chapter 29

Managing Finances and Taxes

CONGRATULATIONS ON YOUR JOURNEY to making millions from YouTube! As your channel continues to grow and generate significant income, it becomes crucial to manage your finances wisely and navigate the complex world of taxes. In this chapter, we will explore key aspects of financial management and provide valuable insights on how to optimize your earnings and stay on top of your tax obligations. Remember, mastering these aspects of your YouTube business is essential for long-term success and financial stability.

Organizing Your Finances

Managing your finances effectively is the foundation for building wealth and ensuring sustainability. Here are some essential steps to help you stay organized:

a. Separate Personal and Business Finances: Open a separate bank account and credit card for your YouTube earnings. This segregation simplifies tracking your business expenses and income, ensuring accurate financial reporting.

b. Maintain Detailed Records: Keep meticulous records of your income, expenses, and any financial transactions related to your YouTube channel. This practice will make tax time less stressful and help you identify areas for potential cost savings.

c. Use Accounting Software: Consider investing in accounting software to streamline your financial management processes. Software options like QuickBooks or Xero can automate tasks, generate reports, and provide a clear snapshot of your financial health.

Budgeting and Expense Management

Creating a comprehensive budget is a vital step toward maintaining financial stability and maximizing your YouTube earnings. To assist you in properly managing your spending, consider the following advice:

a. Track and Analyze Your Expenses: Closely monitor your spending habits and identify areas where you can cut costs. Understanding your cash flow will enable you to allocate resources strategically and reinvest in your channel's growth.

b. Prioritize Investments: Determine which expenses directly contribute to your channel's success. Allocate funds toward equipment upgrades, marketing campaigns, and hiring professionals, such as editors or graphic designers, to enhance your content.

c. Plan for Seasonal Fluctuations: Keep in mind that YouTube ad revenue and brand sponsorships can vary throughout the year. Develop a budget that considers seasonal fluctuations to maintain financial stability during leaner months.

Maximizing Revenue Streams

While YouTube ad revenue is a primary income source, diversifying your revenue streams is essential for long-term financial success. Explore these strategies to maximize your earnings potential:

a. Brand Partnerships and Sponsorships: Collaborate with brands relevant to your niche. Negotiate fair sponsorship deals that align with your values and resonate with your audience. These partnerships can provide substantial additional income.

b. Merchandise and Products: Develop your brand by creating merchandise or digital products such as e-books, courses, or exclusive content for your loyal followers. Launching a well-executed merchandising strategy can be a lucrative source of income.

c. Affiliate Marketing: Leverage your influence by recommending products or services through affiliate marketing programs. You receive a commission when customers use your affiliate links to make purchases. Ensure transparency and only endorse products you genuinely believe in.

d. Crowdfunding and Patreon: Engage with your dedicated fan base by offering exclusive perks or content through crowdfunding platforms like Patreon. Encourage your audience to support your channel financially in exchange for additional benefits.

Tax Considerations and Obligations

As your YouTube channel grows, understanding and fulfilling your tax obligations becomes increasingly important. Consider the following aspects:

a. Consult with a Tax Professional: Engage a qualified tax professional who understands the nuances of YouTuber taxes. They will help you navigate complex tax laws, maximize deductions, and ensure compliance.

b. Classify Your Business Structure: Evaluate whether operating as a sole proprietorship, partnership, LLC, or corporation suits your circumstances best. Each structure carries different tax implications, so seek professional advice to determine the most advantageous option.

c. Record and Report Income Accurately: Keep meticulous records of all your income streams, including YouTube ad revenue, brand partnerships, and merchandise sales. Accurate income reporting is vital for meeting your tax obligations and avoiding penalties.

d. Deductible Expenses: Familiarize yourself with the business expenses you can deduct to minimize your tax liability. Examples include equipment purchases, advertising costs, professional fees, and home office deductions.

e. Quarterly Estimated Taxes: As a self-employed individual, you are responsible for paying quarterly estimated taxes. Consult with your tax professional to determine your estimated tax liability and establish a system for timely payments.

Managing your finances and navigating tax obligations is an essential aspect of building a successful YouTube business. By implementing effective financial strategies, budgeting wisely, diversifying revenue streams, and fulfilling your tax obligations, you can position yourself for long-term financial stability and continued growth. Remember, seeking professional advice and staying informed about the ever-evolving tax landscape are crucial to your financial success. Stay focused, stay organized, and watch your YouTube empire flourish!

As you progress on your journey to making millions from YouTube, ensure you consult with a financial advisor and tax professional to receive personalized advice tailored to your unique circumstances.

Chapter 30

Protecting Your Intellectual Property

In the dynamic world of YouTube, your intellectual property (IP) is one of your most valuable assets. As you continue to make millions from your YouTube channel, it becomes crucial to protect your creative work and safeguard against unauthorized use or infringement. In this chapter, we will explore strategies and best practices to help you protect your intellectual property effectively. By implementing these measures, you can ensure the longevity and profitability of your YouTube business. Let's dive in!

Understand Your Intellectual Property Rights

Before diving into protection strategies, it's essential to understand the different types of intellectual property and the rights associated with each:

a. Copyright: Copyright protects original works of authorship, including videos, music, artwork, and scripts. As the creator, you hold the exclusive rights to reproduce, distribute, perform, and display your copyrighted content.

b. Trademark: Trademarks protect your brand identity, including your channel name, logo, and slogans. Registering a trademark grants you exclusive rights to use and protect these elements, preventing others from using similar marks that may cause confusion.

c. Patents: While less relevant to YouTube creators, patents protect inventions or novel ideas. If you have developed a unique technological or process innovation, you may consider seeking patent protection.

Copyright Protection Strategies

Copyright protection is vital for safeguarding your creative content from unauthorized use or plagiarism. Here are key strategies to protect your copyright:

a. Understand Fair Use: Familiarize yourself with the concept of fair use, which allows limited use of copyrighted material for purposes such as commentary, criticism, parody, or education. While fair use is a defense to copyright infringement, it's crucial to identify and respond to unauthorized use that exceeds fair use boundaries.

b. Copyright Notices: Include a copyright notice in your video descriptions, indicating that your content is protected by copyright. This notice serves as a reminder to viewers and potential infringers that your work is protected.

c. Watermarking: Consider adding a visible watermark to your videos. This serves as a deterrent to unauthorized use and makes it easier to identify your content if it is shared without permission.

d. Register Your Copyright: While copyright protection is automatic upon creation, registering your copyright with the relevant authorities provides additional legal benefits. In many jurisdictions, registration is a prerequisite for filing a lawsuit in case of infringement.

e. Monitor and Enforce: Regularly monitor the internet for unauthorized use of your content. Utilize services like Content ID (YouTube's built-in copyright management tool) or third-party services to identify and take action against infringing uses.

Trademark Protection Strategies

Protecting your brand identity is crucial to maintaining a strong presence on YouTube. Here are strategies to protect your trademarks:

a. Conduct Trademark Searches: Before selecting and using a channel name, logo, or slogan, conduct comprehensive trademark searches to ensure that no conflicting marks already exist. This will help you avoid potential infringement issues in the future.

b. Register Your Trademarks: Registering your trademarks with the appropriate intellectual property office provides you with stronger legal protection and the ability to enforce your rights against infringers. Consult with a trademark attorney to guide you through the registration process.

c. Police and Enforce: Regularly monitor the use of your trademarks and take action against unauthorized use or infringement. Send cease and desist letters when necessary and consider legal action if infringement persists.

Intellectual Property Licensing and Contracts

Licensing your intellectual property allows you to grant others limited rights to use your creative works while maintaining control and generating revenue. Here are important considerations for licensing and contracts:

a. Licensing Agreements: When entering into licensing agreements, clearly define the terms and conditions of use, duration, territories, and royalty arrangements. Consult with an attorney specializing in intellectual property to ensure your rights are protected.

b. Content Collaboration Agreements: If you collaborate with other creators or businesses, establish clear agreements outlining ownership rights, usage permissions, and revenue sharing arrangements.

c. Non-Disclosure Agreements (NDAs): When sharing confidential information or creative ideas, require parties to sign non-disclosure agreements to protect your intellectual property from being shared or used without authorization.

Responding to Intellectual Property Infringement

Despite your best efforts, there may be instances of intellectual property infringement. Here's how to respond effectively:

a. Document Infringements: Keep a record of all instances of infringement, including evidence such as screenshots, timestamps, and relevant URLs. This documentation will support your case if legal action becomes necessary.

b. Cease and Desist Notices: Send a formal cease and desist notice to the infringing party, clearly stating your rights, the infringing activity, and the actions you expect them to take to remedy the situation.

c. DMCA Takedown Notices: Utilize the Digital Millennium Copyright Act (DMCA) takedown process provided by YouTube and other platforms to request the removal of infringing content. Follow the platform's specific guidelines for submitting DMCA notices.

d. Legal Action: If infringement persists or causes significant harm, consult with an intellectual property attorney to assess the feasibility of legal action, including filing a lawsuit for copyright or trademark infringement.

Protecting your intellectual property is essential to safeguarding your creative work and maintaining a thriving YouTube presence. By understanding your intellectual property rights, implementing effective protection strategies, and responding to infringement diligently, you can secure your valuable assets and ensure the longevity and profitability of your YouTube business. Remember, seeking legal advice from professionals specializing in intellectual property law is crucial for comprehensive protection. Stay vigilant, be proactive, and watch your YouTube empire thrive while maintaining control over your intellectual property.

Chapter 31

Dealing with Copyright Issues

CONGRATULATIONS ON YOUR JOURNEY to making millions from YouTube! As you continue to grow your channel and create engaging content, it's essential to understand the complexities of copyright law. Copyright issues can be a stumbling block for many creators, but with the right knowledge and proactive approach, you can navigate this landscape successfully. In this chapter, we will explore the fundamentals of copyright, ways to avoid copyright infringement, and how to respond to copyright claims on YouTube.

Understanding Copyright

Copyright is a legal concept that grants exclusive rights to creators of original works, such as music, videos, literature, and artwork. These rights include the ability to reproduce, distribute, display, and perform the work, as well as create derivative works. Copyright protection arises automatically when an original work is fixed in a tangible medium, such as a video file or written document. It is important to note that copyright law differs between countries, so be mindful of the laws that apply to your jurisdiction.

Avoiding Copyright Infringement

As a content creator, it's crucial to respect the rights of others and avoid infringing on copyrighted material.Certainly! Here are ten tips to help content creators avoid copyright infringement and stay on the right side of the law:

Create Original Content: Focus on developing and producing your own original content. This ensures that you are not using someone else's copyrighted material without permission.

Educate Yourself on Copyright Law: Take the time to understand the basics of copyright law in your jurisdiction. Familiarize yourself with the rights granted to copyright holders and the limitations and exceptions under the law.

Use Royalty-Free or Licensed Material: Utilize royalty-free music, images, and videos that are explicitly designated for commercial use. Alternatively, obtain proper licenses or permissions for copyrighted material you wish to include in your content.

Attribute and Give Credit: If you use third-party content that requires attribution, make sure to provide proper credit to the original creator. This involves naming the author, stating the work's title, and including a hyperlink leading back to the original source.

Explore Creative Commons: Creative Commons licenses offer a range of permissions for creators to share their work with certain conditions. Familiarize yourself with these licenses and use content that aligns with the specific permissions granted.

Understand Fair Use: Educate yourself on the concept of fair use and its application in your jurisdiction. Remember that fair use is a legal defense, and it should be used cautiously and responsibly.

Seek Permission: When in doubt about using copyrighted material, reach out to the copyright owner and ask for explicit permission. This may involve contacting artists, publishers, or other relevant rights holders.

Avoid Parodies and Satire of Copyrighted Works: Parodies and satire can be tricky when it comes to copyright. While they may be protected under fair use, it's best to consult with a legal professional to ensure you are within the boundaries of the law.

Be Mindful of Public Domain: Public domain works are not subject to copyright restrictions and can be freely used. However, be cautious and verify the public domain status of a work before incorporating it into your content.

Regularly Monitor and Audit Your Content: Conduct periodic audits of your content to identify any potential copyright infringements. Keep an eye on your own content as well to prevent unauthorized use by others.

Remember, while these tips can help you avoid copyright infringement, it's always a good idea to consult with a legal professional who specializes in copyright law for specific advice and guidance in your jurisdiction.

Responding to Copyright Claims

Even with the best intentions, you may still encounter copyright claims on your YouTube channel. When this happens, it's essential to handle the situation promptly and professionally. Here's how you can respond effectively:

Familiarize Yourself with YouTube's Copyright Policies: YouTube has a comprehensive set of guidelines and policies regarding copyright infringement. Take the time to understand these policies, as they will provide you with a solid foundation for responding to copyright claims.

Review the Claim: When you receive a copyright claim, carefully review the details provided by the claimant. Determine whether the claim is valid or if you believe it is a mistake or a false claim. Keep in mind that YouTube's Content ID system automatically detects copyrighted material, but it may not always be accurate.

Understand the Options: YouTube offers three options for responding to copyright claims: removing the content, disputing the claim, or monetizing the video with ads for the copyright owner. Consider the specifics of the claim and choose the option that aligns with your goals and legal rights.

Dispute a False Claim: If you believe a copyright claim is incorrect, you can file a dispute. This prompts the claimant to provide evidence supporting their claim or release the copyright claim entirely. However, be cautious when disputing claims, as false or repeated disputes can harm your channel's standing.

Seek Legal Advice: In complex copyright cases or situations where significant revenue or legal consequences are at stake, it's wise to consult with an attorney who specializes in copyright law. They can provide expert guidance and help protect your rights as a content creator.

Dealing with copyright issues is an integral part of being a successful YouTube creator. By understanding copyright law, respecting the rights of others, and responding appropriately to copyright claims, you can navigate this landscape with confidence. Remember to prioritize originality in your content, obtain licenses when necessary, and seek legal advice when facing complex situations. With the right approach, you can continue to make millions from YouTube while respecting the intellectual property of others.

Chapter 32

Handling Controversies and Negative Feedback

IN THE DYNAMIC WORLD of YouTube, controversies and negative feedback are inevitable. As a content creator, it's crucial to understand how to effectively handle these challenges to protect your reputation and continue thriving on the platform. In this chapter, we will explore strategies and techniques to navigate controversies and negative feedback while maintaining a strong presence and monetizing your YouTube channel.

Embrace Constructive Criticism

Negative feedback can be an opportunity for growth and improvement. Instead of shying away from criticism, embrace it as a valuable tool for honing your content. Analyze the feedback objectively, separate personal attacks from genuine critiques, and focus on the areas where you can make meaningful changes. By adopting a receptive mindset, you can turn negative feedback into a catalyst for success.

Stay Calm and Professional

When faced with controversies or negative comments, it's essential to maintain composure and respond in a professional manner. Avoid engaging in heated arguments or exchanging insults with detractors. Remember that your audience is observing your behavior, and responding with grace and professionalism will earn you respect and credibility. Address criticism calmly, provide thoughtful explanations, and express gratitude for feedback, even if it's negative.

Monitor Comments and Respond Appropriately

Monitoring the comments section of your YouTube videos is crucial for identifying controversies and negative feedback. Regularly engage with your viewers, respond to questions, and acknowledge their opinions. However, when facing negative comments or controversies, it's important to respond tactfully. Avoid deleting or hiding negative comments unless they violate YouTube's community guidelines. Instead, address them respectfully and constructively. Engaging in a meaningful conversation can turn critics into supporters.

Apologize and Make Amends

If you make a mistake or unintentionally cause offense, be accountable and offer a sincere apology. Admitting fault and showing remorse can go a long way in rebuilding trust with your audience. Additionally, consider taking corrective actions to rectify the situation. Whether it's revising content, issuing a public statement, or reaching out to affected parties, demonstrating genuine efforts to make amends will exhibit your commitment to growth and improvement.

Focus on Quality Content

One of the most effective ways to counter controversies and negative feedback is by consistently delivering high-quality content. When you prioritize creating valuable and engaging videos, your audience is more likely to overlook minor controversies or negative comments. Concentrate on producing content that aligns with your viewers' expectations, addresses their needs, and brings value to their lives. By staying true to your content's purpose, you can build a loyal following that supports you even during challenging times.

Seek Support from Your Community

Your subscribers and loyal viewers can become a powerful support system during controversies or negative feedback situations. Reach out to your community through community posts, live streams, or social media platforms. Share your thoughts, explain your perspective, and request their understanding. Often, your supporters will come to your defense and counterbalance the negative feedback with positive comments and encouragement.

Collaborate with Peers and Experts

Collaborating with other YouTubers or industry experts can help mitigate controversies and negative feedback. By joining forces with reputable creators, you can tap into their credibility and leverage their influence to address criticism. Seek opportunities to collaborate on videos or participate in discussions that highlight your expertise and showcase your dedication to providing valuable content.

Collaborations can not only boost your channel's reach but also demonstrate your commitment to engaging with different perspectives.

Utilize Privacy and Moderation Tools

YouTube offers various tools and settings that can assist you in handling controversies and negative feedback. Familiarize yourself with these features to effectively manage your channel. Utilize comment moderation to filter out spam and block or hide comments that violate the platform's guidelines. Additionally, consider adjusting privacy settings for certain videos or segments that may attract controversies. Being proactive in utilizing these tools can help create a safer and more positive environment for your audience.

Take a Break and Reflect

When faced with intense controversies or a barrage of negative feedback, it's important to step back and take a break. Give yourself some time to reflect on the situation and assess the validity of the criticism. Use this break to gain perspective, recharge, and regroup. Taking a break doesn't mean ignoring the issue; it means giving yourself space to gather your thoughts and respond in a more composed and strategic manner. Use this time to brainstorm solutions, consult with trusted advisors or fellow creators, and develop a plan of action moving forward.

Transparent Communication

Transparency is key when addressing controversies and negative feedback. Be open and honest with your audience about the situation, explaining your perspective, and sharing your intentions. Clear communication helps build trust and can help diffuse tensions. Consider creating a video or a statement where you address the concerns raised, provide context, and outline your plans for improvement or resolution. By being transparent, you demonstrate your commitment to accountability and invite your audience to be a part of your growth process.

Learn from Past Controversies

Each controversy or negative feedback experience can serve as a valuable learning opportunity. Take the time to evaluate and analyze past controversies to identify patterns or recurring issues. Ask yourself why the controversy arose and what actions you can take to prevent similar situations in the future. Learn from your mistakes and implement strategies to avoid repeating them. This introspection will not only help you handle current controversies but also strengthen your content creation process, ensuring a more positive and successful future for your YouTube channel.

Controversies and negative feedback are part of the YouTube journey, but they don't have to define your success or hinder your growth. By embracing constructive criticism, staying calm and professional, monitoring and responding to comments appropriately, apologizing when necessary, focusing on quality content, seeking support from your community, collaborating with peers and experts, and utilizing privacy and moderation tools, you can effectively handle controversies and negative feedback while continuing to thrive on YouTube.

Remember, setbacks are opportunities for learning and improvement, and with the right approach, you can turn them into stepping stones towards achieving your goals and making millions from YouTube.

Chapter 33

Expanding Your Online Presence Beyond YouTube

Congratulations on successfully building your YouTube channel and mastering the art of content creation! By now, you've likely amassed a dedicated subscriber base and are reaping the rewards of your hard work. However, in order to truly maximize your earning potential and solidify your position as a successful online creator, it's essential to expand your online presence beyond YouTube. In this chapter, we'll explore various strategies and platforms that can help you reach new audiences, diversify your income streams, and continue to grow your brand.

Harness the Power of Social Media

While YouTube is undoubtedly a powerful platform, it's crucial to remember that social media platforms can significantly enhance your online presence. Engaging with your audience on platforms such as Instagram, Twitter, Facebook, and TikTok can help you connect with a broader range of viewers and potential fans. The best way to utilise each platform is as follows:

Instagram: Use Instagram to share behind-the-scenes glimpses, teasers of upcoming videos, and personal insights. Leverage the visual nature of Instagram by posting high-quality photos and engaging with your followers through comments and direct messages.

Twitter: Twitter is a great platform for real-time interactions. Utilize it to share updates, engage in discussions related to your niche, and establish yourself as an authority in your field. Use relevant hashtags and tag other creators or brands to expand your reach.

Facebook: Create a Facebook page for your YouTube channel and regularly post content updates, links to your videos, and exclusive content. Join relevant Facebook groups to engage with a community that shares similar interests.

TikTok: Embrace the short-form video format on TikTok to showcase your creativity and attract a younger demographic. Create entertaining and informative content that aligns with your YouTube channel's theme, and cross-promote your YouTube videos within TikTok.

Remember, consistency is key across all social media platforms. Develop a cohesive brand identity and maintain a regular posting schedule to keep your audience engaged and connected.

Start a Blog or Website

Building a blog or website can serve as an effective hub for your online presence. It provides a centralized location where you can showcase your content, engage with your audience, and monetize your brand. Here are some key steps to get started:

Choose a domain name that reflects your brand and is easy to remember.

Select a reliable web hosting service to ensure your site remains accessible and performs well.

Design an attractive and user-friendly website. Use high-quality visuals, optimize for mobile devices, and make navigation intuitive.

Regularly publish blog posts related to your niche. Offer unique insights, tutorials, or behind-the-scenes stories to provide additional value to your audience.

Utilize search engine optimization (SEO) techniques to increase your website's visibility in search engine results. Research and incorporate relevant keywords into your blog posts, optimize meta tags, and build backlinks from reputable sources.

Incorporate features that encourage audience engagement, such as comments sections, contact forms, and newsletter subscriptions.

A well-maintained blog or website can help establish your authority in your niche, attract new viewers, and provide additional monetization opportunities through affiliate marketing, sponsored content, or selling merchandise.

Explore Podcasting

Podcasting has experienced significant growth in recent years and offers a unique avenue for expanding your online presence. Starting a podcast related to your YouTube channel's content can help you reach a new audience and provide an additional platform for monetization. Consider the following steps to launch a successful podcast:

Choose a podcasting platform and hosting service. Popular options include Anchor, Buzzsprout, and Libsyn.

Define the format and theme of your podcast. Decide whether you'll host it solo or invite guests to provide additional perspectives.

Plan your episodes in advance and create engaging content that complements your YouTube channel.

Invest in a decent microphone and audio editing software to ensure high-quality audio production.

Promote your podcast across various platforms, including your YouTube channel, social media, and website.

Monetize your podcast through sponsorships, advertisements, or by offering exclusive bonus content to paid subscribers.

Podcasting allows you to connect with your audience on a more personal level, share longer-form content, and expand your reach beyond the YouTube platform.

Collaborate with Other Creators

Collaborating with other creators in your niche can be a mutually beneficial strategy for expanding your online presence. Partnering with like-minded creators exposes you to their audience, allowing you to reach new viewers who may become subscribers to your channel. Here are some ways to collaborate effectively:

Identify creators whose content aligns with your own and has a similar target audience. Reach out to them with collaboration proposals that offer value to both parties.

Explore collaboration opportunities such as guest appearances on each other's channels, co-creating content, or participating in challenges together.

Cross-promote each other's content through shout-outs, featured links, or video annotations.

Engage in genuine conversations and interactions with your collaborators to foster a strong and supportive creator community.

Collaborations not only help you expand your reach but also introduce you to new ideas, perspectives, and creative techniques that can enhance your content and keep your audience engaged.

Diversify Revenue Streams

Expanding your online presence beyond YouTube opens up new avenues for generating income. While YouTube's Partner Program and ad revenue can be significant, diversifying your revenue streams provides stability and long-term growth. Consider the following monetization opportunities:

Brand sponsorships: As your online presence grows, brands may approach you for sponsored content. Collaborate with brands that align with your values and create authentic sponsored videos that provide value to your audience.

Affiliate marketing: Promote products or services through affiliate links and earn a commission for each sale made through your referral. Select products relevant to your niche and provide honest recommendations.

Merchandise: Create and sell merchandise related to your brand. This can include clothing, accessories, or even digital products like e-books or online courses.

Paid subscriptions: Offer exclusive content, behind-the-scenes access, or early video releases to subscribers who pay a monthly or yearly fee.

Crowdfunding: Platforms like Patreon or Ko-fi allow your audience to support you directly through donations or recurring payments.

By diversifying your income streams, you'll be less reliant on YouTube's ad revenue and better positioned to sustain and grow your online business.

Expanding your online presence beyond YouTube is a crucial step towards building a robust and sustainable online brand. Utilize social media platforms, start a blog or website, explore podcasting, collaborate with other creators, and diversify your income streams. Remember, the key to success lies in consistency, authenticity, and providing value to your audience. Embrace these strategies, adapt them to your unique brand, and watch your online presence thrive beyond YouTube.

Part VI

Diversifying Income and Long-Term Success

Chapter 34

Creating and Selling Digital Products

IN THIS CHAPTER, WE will delve into the exciting world of creating and selling digital products. As a successful YouTuber, you already have a dedicated audience that trusts and values your content. Now, it's time to leverage that audience and turn your expertise into profitable digital products. Whether you're a gamer, a beauty guru, or a vlogger, there are countless opportunities to create and sell digital products that resonate with your audience and generate substantial revenue. Let's explore the strategies and steps involved in this lucrative endeavor.

Understanding the Power of Digital Products

Digital products offer a scalable and low-cost way to monetize your YouTube channel. Unlike physical products, digital products can be created once and sold repeatedly without the need for inventory or shipping. Some popular digital products include eBooks, online courses, presets, templates, stock footage, and music tracks. These products provide value to your audience while allowing you to generate passive income.

Identifying Your Niche

To create successful digital products, it's crucial to understand your niche and target audience. Consider the interests and needs of your viewers. What challenges do they face? What knowledge or skills can you offer to help them overcome those challenges? By aligning your digital products with your niche, you can ensure a higher conversion rate and customer satisfaction.

Conducting Market Research

Before diving into product creation, conduct thorough market research to validate your product idea. Look for existing digital products in your niche and analyze their popularity, pricing, and customer reviews. This research will help you identify gaps in the market and ensure that your product stands out from the competition.

Brainstorming Product Ideas

Once you have a clear understanding of your niche and the market, brainstorm product ideas that align with your expertise and audience's needs. Consider the format that best suits your content, such as eBooks, video courses, or software tools. Don't be afraid to think outside the box and innovate within your niche. Unique and valuable products have a higher chance of success.

Creating High-Quality Content

The success of your digital products hinges on the quality of the content you provide. Invest time and effort in creating comprehensive, well-researched, and visually appealing products. Whether it's an eBook or an online course, ensure that the content is engaging, informative, and delivers on its promises. You want your customers to feel that they've received excellent value for their money.

Choosing the Right Platform

Selecting the right platform to sell your digital products is vital. Popular options include self-hosted websites, e-commerce platforms, and online marketplaces. Each platform has its pros and cons, so consider factors such as ease of use, customization options, transaction fees, and marketing capabilities. Evaluate which platform aligns best with your goals and budget.

When it comes to choosing the right platform to sell your digital products, there are several options available that align with different goals and budgets. Here are 10 popular platforms that you can consider:

Shopify: Shopify is a leading e-commerce platform that offers a user-friendly interface and a wide range of customization options. It allows you to set up your own online store, manage inventory, and integrate various payment gateways. While there are monthly fees associated with using Shopify, it provides a robust set of features for selling digital products.

WooCommerce: If you already have a WordPress website, WooCommerce is an excellent choice. It is a plugin that transforms your WordPress site into an e-commerce platform. WooCommerce offers flexibility, customization options, and seamless integration with WordPress. You can sell both physical and digital products and have control over your store's design and functionality.

Gumroad: Gumroad is a popular platform for selling digital products such as eBooks, videos, and music. It provides a simple and intuitive interface, making it easy to upload and sell your products. Gumroad handles payment processing and allows you to customize the look of your product pages. It also provides marketing tools and analytics to help you optimize your sales.

SendOwl: A platform called SendOwl was created exclusively for the sale of digital goods. It offers features like automated product delivery, customizable purchase buttons, and secure payment processing. SendOwl supports a variety of file types and has options for upselling, affiliate marketing, and customer management.

Teachable: If you're interested in creating and selling online courses, Teachable is an excellent platform to consider. It provides a comprehensive course creation interface with options for multimedia content, quizzes, and certificates. Teachable also handles payment processing, student management, and provides marketing tools to help you promote your courses.

Podia: Selling online courses, digital downloads, and memberships are all possible with Podia's all-in-one platform. It offers an intuitive interface for creating and managing your products. Podia also provides features like email marketing, affiliate marketing, and a customizable storefront to showcase your products.

Etsy: While Etsy is primarily known as a marketplace for handmade and vintage items, it also allows you to sell digital products. If your digital products have a creative or craft-related focus, Etsy can be a great platform to reach a large audience interested in unique and artistic content.

Payhip: Payhip is a straightforward platform for selling digital products. It supports various file types, provides secure payment processing, and offers options for discounts and promotional campaigns. Payhip also has a built-in affiliate program, making it easier to collaborate with influencers and expand your reach.

Selz: Selz is an e-commerce platform that caters to both physical and digital products. It offers features such as customizable storefronts, secure payment processing, and integrations with popular email marketing tools. Selz also provides analytics and reporting to help you track your sales and optimize your marketing efforts.

E-junkie: E-junkie is a platform that specializes in selling digital downloads, including eBooks, music, software, and more. It offers secure product delivery, supports multiple payment gateways, and provides features for managing affiliates and discount codes. E-junkie is known for its simplicity and affordability.

Remember to evaluate each platform based on your specific needs, budget, and long-term goals. Consider factors like pricing, ease of use, customization options, payment processing, and marketing capabilities to determine which platform aligns best with your business objectives.

Setting an Appropriate Price:

Pricing your digital products can be challenging. It's essential to strike a balance between generating revenue and making your products accessible to your target audience. Consider factors such as production costs, market demand, competition, and perceived value. Offering different pricing tiers or bundles can also appeal to a wider range of customers.

Building an Effective Sales Funnel

To maximize your digital product sales, create a well-defined sales funnel. A sales funnel consists of a series of steps that guide potential customers from discovering your product to making a purchase. This can include opt-in forms, lead magnets, email marketing, and upsells. By nurturing relationships with your audience and providing value at each stage, you can significantly increase your conversion rate.

Promoting Your Digital Products

Promotion is crucial for driving sales and gaining visibility for your digital products. Leverage your existing YouTube channel to promote your products through engaging and informative videos. Utilize your social media platforms, email list, and collaborations with other content creators to expand your reach. Consider running targeted ads to reach new audiences who may be interested in your niche.

Engaging with Your Customers

Providing excellent customer support and engagement is essential for building a loyal customer base. Respond to inquiries promptly, address any concerns, and seek feedback from your customers. This interaction not only enhances customer satisfaction but also helps you refine your products based on their needs and preferences.

Scaling Your Digital Product Business

As your digital product business grows, explore opportunities to scale your operations. This can include outsourcing certain tasks, automating processes, or expanding your product line. To stay ahead of the competition and meet the changing needs of your audience, you must constantly assess and improve your methods.

Creating and selling digital products is a powerful way to monetize your YouTube channel and generate significant revenue. By understanding your niche, conducting market research, and providing high-quality content, you can create products that resonate with your audience. Utilize effective sales funnels, promotional strategies, and customer engagement techniques to maximize your sales. Remember, the key to success lies in consistently delivering value to your customers and adapting to the ever-changing digital landscape. Good luck on your journey to creating and selling digital products!

Chapter 35

Writing Books and Publishing eBooks

WRITING BOOKS AND PUBLISHING eBooks

Writing a book is an incredible opportunity to share your knowledge, insights, and experiences with a wide audience. In the digital age, publishing eBooks has become increasingly popular and accessible, providing aspiring authors with a platform to reach millions of readers worldwide. In this chapter, we will explore the process of writing books and publishing eBooks, with a focus on leveraging your success on YouTube to maximize your potential for making millions.

Section 1: The Power of Books

The Importance of Books

Books have a timeless appeal that surpasses technological trends. They offer a unique opportunity to delve deep into a subject, present a cohesive narrative, and engage readers in a profound way.

While YouTube allows for visual and audio content, books provide a different medium through which you can connect with your audience on a more personal level. A well-crafted book can establish your authority, expand your brand, and open doors to new opportunities.

Leveraging YouTube for Book Success

As a successful YouTube creator, you already have a built-in audience that is interested in your content. By tapping into this existing fan base, you can significantly increase your chances of book success. Utilize your YouTube channel to promote your upcoming book, offer sneak peeks, and create anticipation among your subscribers. Consider hosting live Q&A sessions or contests to involve your audience in the book writing process. Engage with your viewers and build excitement around your book release.

Section 2: Writing Your Book

Choosing a Topic

Selecting the right topic for your book is crucial. It should align with your expertise and cater to the interests of your target audience. Consider the topics you have covered on your YouTube channel and identify areas where you can provide deeper insights or expand upon existing content. Conduct market research to understand the demand for your chosen topic and ensure there is an audience eager to consume your book.

Outlining and Structuring Your Book

Before diving into the writing process, create a detailed outline that will serve as a roadmap for your book. Divide it into chapters and sections, organizing your content logically and coherently. Each chapter should have a clear purpose and flow smoothly into the next. Remember to include an introduction and conclusion to provide a comprehensive reading experience. A well-structured book will help you maintain focus and guide your readers effectively.

Writing Engaging Content

Writing compelling content is essential to captivate your readers. Develop your unique writing style, one that reflects your personality and resonates with your audience. Use storytelling techniques to engage readers emotionally and keep them invested in your book. Balance factual information with anecdotes, case studies, and real-life examples to make your content relatable and memorable. Maintain a conversational tone to ensure accessibility and avoid overly technical language.

Editing and Proofreading

Editing and proofreading are critical steps in the book writing process. It is recommended to enlist the help of a professional editor or proofreader to ensure your book is free from grammatical errors, typos, and inconsistencies. A well-edited book enhances its credibility and increases the likelihood of positive reviews and word-of-mouth recommendations. Take the time to review and revise your content multiple times to polish your writing and deliver a high-quality book.

Section 3: Publishing Your eBook

Self-Publishing vs. Traditional Publishing

In today's digital landscape, self-publishing offers numerous advantages over traditional publishing. Self-publishing allows you to retain creative control, set your own pricing, and earn higher royalties. It also provides a faster time-to-market and allows for frequent updates and revisions. However, traditional publishing offers the benefits of an established publishing house's marketing and distribution resources. Consider your goals, resources, and preferences when deciding between self-publishing and traditional publishing.

Choosing the Right eBook Platform

When self-publishing an eBook, selecting the right platform is crucial. Platforms like Amazon Kindle Direct Publishing (KDP), Smashwords, and Apple Books offer user-friendly interfaces, global distribution, and royalty tracking systems. Research each platform's terms, features, and reach to determine the best fit for your book. Consider utilizing multiple platforms to maximize your book's visibility and potential earnings.

When it comes to self-publishing an eBook and maximizing its visibility and potential earnings, it's important to consider multiple platforms. Here are ten platforms you can explore:

Amazon Kindle Direct Publishing (KDP): As the largest eBook platform, KDP offers extensive reach and powerful marketing tools. It provides global distribution and allows you to tap into Amazon's vast customer base.

Smashwords: Smashwords offers distribution to multiple eBook retailers, including Barnes & Noble, Apple Books, and Kobo. It provides a user-friendly interface and comprehensive sales reporting.

Apple Books: Apple Books is the eBook platform for iOS devices. Publishing on Apple Books allows you to reach a significant number of readers using Apple devices such as iPhones, iPads, and Macs.

Barnes & Noble Press: Barnes & Noble Press (formerly known as Nook Press) enables you to publish and distribute eBooks on Barnes & Noble's platform. It caters to a dedicated eBook reader audience.

Kobo Writing Life: Kobo is a popular eBook retailer with a global presence, particularly in Canada and Europe. Kobo Writing Life allows you to publish your eBook directly on their platform.

Google Play Books: Google Play Books offers a vast audience of Android users. By publishing your eBook on this platform, you can reach readers who prefer Android devices and enjoy Google's extensive distribution network.

Draft2Digital: Draft2Digital is a platform that simplifies the eBook distribution process. It enables you to publish your eBook across multiple platforms, including Kobo, Apple Books, Barnes & Noble, and more, saving you time and effort.

Lulu: Lulu provides a self-publishing platform for both eBooks and print-on-demand books. It offers a wide range of distribution options, including major online retailers and brick-and-mortar bookstores.

BookBaby: BookBaby is a comprehensive self-publishing platform that offers eBook distribution, printing services, and marketing tools. It provides access to various eBook retailers and libraries.

Scribd: Scribd is a subscription-based platform that allows readers unlimited access to a vast library of eBooks. Publishing your eBook on Scribd exposes it to their subscriber base and increases its discoverability.

Remember to research each platform's terms, features, royalty rates, and reach before making a decision. It may be beneficial to choose a combination of platforms to expand your eBook's visibility and attract a diverse readership.

Formatting Your eBook

Proper formatting is essential for a seamless reading experience. Ensure your eBook is compatible with various devices and screen sizes by using industry-standard formats such as EPUB and MOBI. Pay attention to font styles, sizes, spacing, and formatting elements like headings, subheadings, and bullet points. Include a visually appealing cover that accurately represents your book's content and attracts potential readers.

Marketing and Promoting Your eBook

Marketing and promotion are vital to maximize the reach of your eBook. Leverage your YouTube channel to promote your book to your existing audience. Create engaging promotional content, such as book trailers or behind-the-scenes videos, to generate excitement. Utilize social media platforms, email newsletters, and guest blogging opportunities to expand your reach beyond your YouTube subscribers. Consider offering limited-time discounts or hosting virtual book launches to attract new readers.

Writing books and publishing eBooks provide tremendous opportunities to expand your influence, connect with a broader audience, and generate additional revenue. By leveraging your success on YouTube and following the steps outlined in this chapter, you can increase your chances of making millions through book sales. Remember to choose a compelling topic, write engaging content, and effectively market your eBook to maximize your success as an author. Embrace the power of books and unleash your creativity to leave a lasting impact on your readers.

Chapter 36

Public Speaking and Hosting Events

Public speaking and hosting events can be powerful tools for YouTube creators looking to expand their reach, connect with their audience on a deeper level, and even monetize their channel further. In this chapter, we will explore the art of public speaking, event hosting, and how to leverage these skills to make millions from YouTube. From honing your speaking abilities to organizing successful events, we will cover everything you need to know to captivate your audience and create memorable experiences.

Section 1: Developing Your Public Speaking Skills

Overcoming Stage Fright

Public speaking can be intimidating, but with the right mindset and preparation, you can conquer stage fright. Start by understanding that nervousness is normal and can even enhance your performance. Practice deep breathing exercises, visualize success, and gradually expose yourself to speaking in front of larger audiences. Remember, confidence comes with experience.

Crafting a Compelling Speech

A compelling speech captures your audience's attention and leaves a lasting impact. Begin by outlining your main points and organizing them logically. Use storytelling, humor, and relatable anecdotes to engage your audience emotionally. Practice your speech repeatedly to improve your delivery and ensure a smooth flow. Utilize vocal variety, gestures, and eye contact to enhance your overall presence.

Building Authentic Connection

Connecting with your audience is essential for effective public speaking. Be authentic, genuine, and relatable in your delivery. Show vulnerability when appropriate and share personal experiences that resonate with your viewers. Engage with your audience by asking questions, encouraging participation, and addressing their concerns. The more connected they feel to you, the more likely they are to support your channel.

Section 2: Leveraging Public Speaking for YouTube Success

Collaborative Speaking Engagements

Collaborating with other influencers and experts in your niche can amplify your reach and credibility. Seek opportunities to participate in panel discussions, conferences, or industry events as a speaker. Share your expertise, network with fellow creators, and leverage these engagements to cross-promote your YouTube channel. By associating yourself with other influential individuals, you can expand your subscriber base and attract new viewers.

Hosting Workshops and Masterclasses

Hosting workshops and masterclasses allows you to share your knowledge and establish yourself as an authority in your field. Identify a topic that aligns with your channel's niche and create a valuable learning experience for your audience. Promote these events through your YouTube channel, social media platforms, and email list. Charging a fee for these workshops can generate additional revenue streams while showcasing your expertise.

Speaking Engagements as Content

Record your speaking engagements and repurpose them as content for your YouTube channel. Edit the footage to create shorter, engaging videos that offer insights and highlights from your speech. This allows you to reach a wider audience and provide valuable content while showcasing your public speaking abilities. Don't forget to optimize these videos with relevant keywords and engaging titles to attract more viewers.

Section 3: Organizing Memorable Events

Identifying the Purpose and Target Audience

When hosting an event, clearly define its purpose and identify your target audience. Determine whether it will be a fan meetup, a live show, a charity event, or a combination. Understand your audience's preferences, interests, and expectations to tailor the event experience accordingly. Research successful events in your industry to gather inspiration and incorporate unique elements that align with your brand.

Planning and Logistics

Planning is key to hosting a successful event. Start by establishing a budget, securing a venue, and creating a detailed timeline. Consider the technical requirements, such as audiovisual equipment, lighting, and seating arrangements. Collaborate with sponsors, vendors, or partners to enhance the event experience and generate additional revenue streams. Develop a comprehensive marketing strategy to promote the event and generate excitement among your audience.

Engaging and Interactive Experiences

Make your event memorable by incorporating engaging and interactive experiences. Offer Q&A sessions, live performances, demonstrations, or interactive workshops related to your YouTube content. Encourage audience participation through contests, giveaways, and meet-and-greets. Foster a sense of community by providing opportunities for attendees to connect with each other and with you personally.

Monetization Opportunities

Events provide various monetization opportunities beyond ticket sales. Consider offering premium ticket packages that include exclusive merchandise, backstage access, or private sessions with you. Collaborate with sponsors to secure brand partnerships, product placements, or event sponsorships. Explore opportunities for live streaming the event to generate additional revenue from virtual attendees who couldn't attend in person.

Public speaking and hosting events offer YouTube creators powerful avenues to engage with their audience, expand their reach, and monetize their channel further. By developing your public speaking skills, leveraging speaking engagements for YouTube success, and organizing memorable events, you can create unique experiences that leave a lasting impact on your viewers. Embrace these opportunities, be authentic, and continue refining your craft to build a loyal and engaged community while making millions from YouTube.

Chapter 37

Licensing and Syndication Opportunities

IN THIS CHAPTER, WE will delve into the exciting world of licensing and syndication opportunities. As a successful YouTuber, your content has the potential to reach a massive audience, and licensing and syndication can help you unlock new revenue streams while expanding your brand's reach. This chapter will guide you through the process of exploring, negotiating, and maximizing these opportunities to make the most of your YouTube success.

Understanding Licensing

Licensing involves granting permission to others to use your content in exchange for a fee or a percentage of the revenue generated. By licensing your videos, you can tap into various mediums such as television, film, commercials, documentaries, and more. Licensing allows you to extend your content's lifespan and reach audiences beyond YouTube's platform, opening up new avenues for income and recognition.

Identifying Licensing Opportunities

Research Potential Partners: Start by researching potential licensing partners who align with your content and brand. Look for production companies, advertising agencies, and streaming platforms that may be interested in leveraging your content for their projects. Make a list of potential partners and assess their credibility, track record, and compatibility with your brand.

Contact Licensing Agencies: Reach out to licensing agencies specializing in connecting content creators with licensing opportunities. These agencies have existing relationships with industry professionals and can help match your content with the right partners. They can also negotiate on your behalf, ensuring that you receive fair compensation for the use of your content.

Leverage Your Network: Use your existing connections within the industry to explore licensing opportunities. Attend conferences, networking events, and trade shows to meet industry professionals who may be interested in collaborating with you. Building relationships and leveraging your network can lead to exciting licensing opportunities that you may not have discovered otherwise.

Negotiating Licensing Agreements:

Establish Clear Terms: When negotiating licensing agreements, it's crucial to establish clear terms that outline the scope of usage, duration, and compensation. Ensure that the agreement protects your rights as the content creator and clearly defines how your content will be used. Seek legal advice if necessary to ensure that the terms are fair and favorable to you.

Determine Pricing and Royalties: Determine the pricing structure and royalties for licensing your content. Factors such as the medium of usage, audience reach, and exclusivity will influence the pricing. Consider both upfront fees and ongoing royalties, ensuring that you are adequately compensated for the value your content brings.

Retain Ownership and Control: It's important to retain ownership and control over your content when entering into licensing agreements. Maintain the right to review and approve any edits or modifications made to your videos. Also, specify any restrictions on the usage of your content to protect your brand and ensure its integrity is maintained.

Exploring Syndication Opportunities:

Syndication involves distributing your content to multiple platforms or publishers in exchange for a share of the advertising revenue generated. Syndicating your videos allows you to expand your reach to new audiences while monetizing your content through advertising partnerships.

Collaborate with Multi-Channel Networks (MCNs): Multi-Channel Networks are companies that partner with content creators to help manage their YouTube channels and explore syndication opportunities. MCNs have established relationships with advertisers and can negotiate better revenue-sharing agreements for your content. Research reputable MCNs and consider joining forces with them to maximize your syndication opportunities.

Partner with Online Video Platforms: Expand your reach by partnering with online video platforms that cater to your target audience. Platforms like Vevo, Vessel, or Dailymotion provide alternative avenues to showcase your content and monetize it through advertising. Research these platforms, evaluate their reach and audience demographics, and consider partnering with those that align with your content and goals.

Negotiating Syndication Deals: When negotiating syndication deals, consider factors such as revenue sharing percentages, ad placement control, and exclusivity. Ensure that you retain control over where and how advertisements are displayed on your videos. Look for syndication partners who can offer competitive revenue-sharing models and access to a large and engaged audience.

Utilize Social Media Platforms: Extend your syndication efforts by leveraging social media platforms to distribute and promote your content. Platforms like Facebook Watch, Instagram IGTV, and Snapchat Discover offer opportunities to reach new audiences and monetize your videos through advertising partnerships. Explore partnerships or syndication opportunities specific to each platform and tailor your content to their formats and audience preferences.

Explore Traditional Media Outlets: Syndication opportunities are not limited to online platforms. Traditional media outlets such as television networks, radio stations, and print publications may be interested in featuring or repurposing your content. Reach out to media outlets that align with your niche or target audience, and explore potential collaborations or licensing agreements to expand your reach beyond the digital realm.

Engage in Content Swaps and Collaborations: Consider engaging in content swaps or collaborations with other content creators or channels that have a complementary audience. By cross-promoting each other's content, you can expand your reach and tap into new audiences that may be interested in your videos. Collaborations can also lead to syndication opportunities as you leverage each other's networks and expertise.

Develop Branded Content Partnerships: Branded content partnerships involve creating sponsored or co-branded videos in collaboration with brands or advertisers. These partnerships can provide a significant source of revenue while allowing you to reach new audiences. Seek out brands that align with your content and audience demographics, and negotiate mutually beneficial partnerships that maintain the authenticity of your content.

Explore International Syndication Opportunities: Syndicating your content internationally can open up a whole new world of opportunities. Research platforms and media outlets in different countries that may be interested in licensing or syndicating your videos. Consider translating or localizing your content to cater to specific international markets and engage with local audiences.

Leverage Live Streaming Platforms: Live streaming platforms such as Twitch or Facebook Live offer unique syndication opportunities. By streaming your content live on these platforms, you can tap into their existing user base and monetize through donations, subscriptions, or ad revenue. Explore partnerships or syndication deals specific to live streaming platforms and consider integrating live streaming into your content strategy.

Create Exclusive Content for Subscription-Based Platforms: Subscription-based platforms like Patreon or OnlyFans allow you to create exclusive content for your most dedicated fans. By offering premium content or behind-the-scenes access, you can monetize your loyal audience while maintaining a more intimate connection. Research subscription-based platforms that align with your content and explore syndication or partnership opportunities with them.

Syndication opportunities provide content creators with a multitude of avenues to expand their reach, monetize their content, and connect with new audiences. Licensing and syndication opportunities can significantly enhance your revenue potential as a YouTube content creator. By exploring licensing agreements and syndication partnerships, you can extend your content's reach to new platforms and audiences while monetizing your videos beyond YouTube's ad revenue.

Remember to thoroughly research potential partners, negotiate favorable terms, and retain control over your content throughout the process. Embrace these opportunities as they arise and continue to create compelling content that resonates with your audience, opening up new doors for success in the ever-evolving world of digital media.

Chapter 38

Investing and Growing Your Wealth

CONGRATULATIONS ON YOUR SUCCESS as a YouTuber! By this point, you've learned how to create engaging content, build a substantial subscriber base, and monetize your channel effectively. Now, it's time to explore a crucial aspect of your journey: investing and growing your wealth. In this chapter, we will delve into strategies and insights that can help you make the most of your earnings and build a solid financial future.

The Importance of Investing

As your YouTube channel grows and generates income, it's vital to recognize that investing is not just an option, but a necessity. While the money you make from your channel is undoubtedly exciting, it's crucial to allocate your funds wisely to ensure long-term financial security. Investing allows your money to work for you, creating additional income streams and multiplying your wealth over time.

Educate Yourself

Before diving into the world of investing, take the time to educate yourself. Read books, follow reputable financial blogs, and attend seminars or workshops on investing. Building a solid foundation of knowledge will help you make informed decisions and navigate the complex investment landscape with confidence.

Set Clear Financial Goals

To develop a successful investment strategy, it's essential to establish clear financial goals. What do you want to achieve with your wealth? Whether it's funding a dream home, saving for retirement, or starting a new business, defining your objectives will guide your investment decisions and help you stay focused.

Diversify Your Portfolio

When it comes to investing, diversification is key. Divide your money among various asset groups, including equities, bonds, real estate, and commodities. This diversification helps reduce risk by ensuring that a single investment does not overly impact your overall portfolio. Additionally, consider diversifying geographically by investing in both domestic and international markets.

Seek Professional Guidance

While educating yourself is crucial, seeking professional guidance is equally important. A financial advisor or investment manager can provide valuable insights tailored to your specific financial situation and goals. They can help you identify suitable investment opportunities, manage your portfolio, and make adjustments as needed.

Remember to choose a reputable advisor who has your best interests at heart.

Long-Term Investing Mindset

Investing is not a get-rich-quick scheme; it requires patience and a long-term mindset. Avoid being swayed by short-term market fluctuations or trying to time the market. Instead, focus on long-term trends and invest in assets that have the potential for sustained growth. By staying invested over time, you allow compounding to work its magic and maximize your returns.

Regularly Review and Rebalance

The continual process of investing necessitates regular portfolio reviews and rebalancing. Markets change, and your financial goals may evolve, so it's essential to reassess your investments periodically. Evaluate the performance of each asset class and make adjustments as necessary to ensure your portfolio remains aligned with your objectives.

Consider Real Estate Investments

Real estate can be an excellent avenue for growing your wealth. ook at possibilities like rental homes, business properties, or real estate investment trusts (REITs). Real estate investments provide the potential for rental income, capital appreciation, and tax advantages. However, thorough research and due diligence are essential to mitigate risks and maximize returns.

Embrace Technology

As a YouTuber, you're already familiar with the power of technology. Embrace it in your investment journey as well. Consider using online investment platforms that offer low fees, user-friendly interfaces, and access to a wide range of investment options. Robo-advisors, for example, use algorithms to manage your investments automatically based on your risk tolerance and goals.

Stay Informed and Adapt

The investment landscape is ever-evolving, so it's crucial to stay informed and adapt accordingly. Keep up with financial news, follow industry trends, and be aware of changes in regulations that may impact your investments. By staying proactive and knowledgeable, you can make informed decisions and seize opportunities that align with your financial goals.

Philanthropy and Giving Back

As your wealth grows, consider incorporating philanthropy into your financial plan. Giving back to causes you care about not only makes a positive impact on society but can also provide personal fulfillment. Explore charitable giving options, establish a foundation, or support existing organizations that align with your values. Remember, generosity has a way of coming back to you in unexpected ways.

Invest in Yourself: Continuous Learning and Skill Development

As a YouTuber, investing in yourself is crucial for long-term success. Allocate resources to continuously learn and develop new skills that can enhance your content creation abilities, expand your knowledge in your niche, and stay ahead of the competition. Consider investing in courses, workshops, or mentorship programs that can help you refine your craft, improve your production quality, or explore new creative avenues. By investing in yourself, you'll be better equipped to adapt to industry changes and seize emerging opportunities.

Take Advantage of Tax Strategies and Financial Instruments

When it comes to growing your wealth, it's essential to be aware of tax strategies and financial instruments that can optimize your earnings. Consult with a tax professional or financial advisor who can guide you in understanding tax-efficient investment vehicles such as Individual Retirement Accounts (IRAs), 401(k) plans, or tax-deferred savings accounts. These instruments can help minimize your tax liability while allowing your investments to grow over time. Additionally, explore tax deductions and credits available to content creators, such as deductions for business expenses related to your channel, equipment purchases, or home office expenses.

Consider Passive Income Opportunities

While YouTube revenue can be a significant source of income, exploring passive income opportunities can provide additional financial stability and growth. Passive income streams require initial effort and investment but can generate recurring revenue with minimal ongoing effort. Explore options such as creating and selling digital products like e-books, online courses, or merchandise related to your channel. You can also consider affiliate marketing, where you earn a commission by promoting products or services that align with your content. By diversifying your income streams, you create a more robust financial foundation and reduce dependence on a single revenue source.

Mitigate Risks: Emergency Funds and Insurance

Building and protecting your wealth also require a focus on risk management. In order to provide a form of security in case of unforeseen financial losses, it is imperative to establish an emergency fund. Save three to six months' worth of spending for a comfortable lifestyle in a separate account. Additionally, consider insurance options to protect yourself and your assets. Health insurance, disability insurance, and liability insurance can provide financial security and peace of mind. Analyze your specific needs and consult with an insurance professional to ensure you have adequate coverage based on your circumstances.

Investing is a vital component of growing and preserving your wealth as a successful YouTuber. By educating yourself, setting clear goals, diversifying your portfolio, seeking professional guidance, and embracing a long-term mindset, you can navigate the investment landscape with confidence. Remember to regularly review and rebalance your portfolio, consider real estate investments, embrace technology, and stay informed to adapt to changing market conditions. Finally, consider incorporating philanthropy into your financial plan to make a positive impact on others while enjoying personal fulfilment. With dedication, knowledge, and a strategic approach, you can turn your YouTube success into a lasting financial legacy.

Part VII

Staying Informed and Adapting to Changes

Chapter 39

Keeping Up with YouTube Policies and Guidelines

In the ever-evolving world of YouTube, staying up to date with its policies and guidelines is crucial for creators who aspire to make millions from their channels. YouTube's policies and guidelines provide the framework for content creation, ensuring a safe and enjoyable experience for users. In this chapter, we will delve into the importance of understanding and adhering to these policies, and provide you with practical tips on how to navigate them effectively.

Section 1: The Role of YouTube Policies

Creating a Safe Environment

YouTube is committed to maintaining a safe environment for its users, and its policies reflect this commitment. By enforcing guidelines regarding harmful or dangerous content, hate speech, harassment, and violence, YouTube aims to protect both creators and viewers. Understanding these policies is vital to ensure your content aligns with YouTube's expectations.

Compliance with Legal Requirements

YouTube is legally bound to enforce certain policies to comply with local laws and regulations. These policies cover areas such as copyright infringement, privacy rights, and child safety. Familiarizing yourself with these guidelines will help you avoid legal troubles and maintain a positive reputation on the platform.

Section 2: Understanding YouTube's Community Guidelines

Creating and Sharing Content

YouTube's Community Guidelines outline the acceptable types of content and behaviors on the platform. These guidelines cover a wide range of topics, including hate speech, violence, nudity, spam, scams, and misleading information. Familiarize yourself with these guidelines to ensure your content meets the platform's standards.

Avoiding Copyright Infringement

YouTube takes copyright infringement seriously and has robust policies in place to protect intellectual property rights. Understand how to use copyrighted material legally, such as obtaining proper licenses or using content under fair use. Additionally, learn how to avoid using copyrighted material without permission, as it can lead to penalties and even account termination.

Section 3: Adherence to YouTube's Monetization Policies

Eligibility for Monetization

YouTube's Partner Program enables creators to earn revenue from their content. However, there are certain eligibility requirements and policies to fulfill. These include having at least 1,000 subscribers, 4,000 watch hours in the past 12 months, adhering to all YouTube policies, and living in a region where the program is available. Stay updated on these policies to ensure you qualify for monetization.

Ad-Friendly Content

YouTube's monetization policies also emphasize creating ad-friendly content. Adsense, YouTube's advertising platform, prefers to associate with content that is suitable for all audiences. Understanding what constitutes ad-friendly content, such as avoiding excessive violence, profanity, or controversial topics, can help maximize your revenue potential.

Section 4: Staying Informed and Navigating Policy Changes

YouTube Help Center

YouTube provides a comprehensive Help Center that serves as a valuable resource for understanding its policies. The Help Center offers detailed explanations, examples, and clarifications regarding the platform's guidelines. Regularly consult this resource to familiarize yourself with YouTube's latest policies and any updates or changes that may occur.

Creator Insider and YouTube News

YouTube actively communicates with its creator community through channels such as the Creator Insider and YouTube News. These platforms provide updates on policy changes, new features, and best practices. Subscribing to these channels or following them on social media can keep you informed about the latest policy developments.

YouTube Studio Notifications

YouTube Studio, the platform's dashboard for creators, provides notifications regarding policy violations, copyright claims, and other important updates. Regularly check your YouTube Studio dashboard to stay informed about any policy-related issues with your content.

Section 5: Handling Policy Violations and Strikes

Understanding Strikes and Penalties:

YouTube has a system of strikes and penalties in place to enforce its policies. When a creator violates a policy, they may receive a strike on their channel. Understanding the different types of strikes, such as community guidelines strikes and copyright strikes, is crucial. Each strike carries specific consequences, such as content removal, loss of monetization, or channel termination. Familiarize yourself with the strike system to avoid violations and effectively address any issues that may arise.

Appealing and Resolving Policy Violations

In the event that you receive a strike or face a policy violation, it's important to know how to handle the situation. YouTube provides an appeals process that allows creators to contest strikes and provide additional context or evidence. Familiarize yourself with the appeals process and follow the necessary steps to resolve policy violations. Promptly addressing and rectifying any issues can help protect your channel's reputation and ensure its continued growth.

Section 6: Promoting a Positive and Engaged Community

Encouraging Positive Engagement

YouTube values a positive and engaged community. Encourage constructive discussions and interactions with your viewers by actively moderating comments, responding to feedback, and fostering a welcoming environment. Uphold YouTube's policies on harassment, hate speech, and cyberbullying to create a safe and inclusive space for your audience.

Collaborating with YouTube's Features

YouTube offers various features that can enhance community engagement and strengthen your channel. Utilize features such as live streaming, community posts, and YouTube Premieres to connect with your audience in real-time and build anticipation for new content. Familiarize yourself with the guidelines and best practices for utilizing these features effectively.

Section 7: Proactive Measures to Avoid Policy Issues

Content Planning and Research

To minimize the risk of policy violations, it's essential to plan your content thoughtfully and conduct thorough research. Understand the guidelines related to the topics you plan to cover, ensuring they align with YouTube's policies. Take the time to research copyright restrictions, trademarks, and permissions when using external content or references. By proactively addressing potential issues during the content planning stage, you can reduce the likelihood of policy violations.

Regular Content Audits

Performing regular audits of your content can help identify any potential policy violations or areas for improvement. Review your videos, titles, descriptions, and thumbnails to ensure they comply with YouTube's guidelines. Additionally, use the YouTube Analytics tool to monitor viewer engagement and feedback, adjusting your content strategy accordingly. By regularly assessing and refining your content, you can maintain a channel that aligns with YouTube's policies and resonates with your audience.

Section 8: Seeking Legal Advice and Professional Support

Consulting Legal Professionals

If you encounter complex legal issues related to copyright, privacy, or other areas, it may be beneficial to seek legal advice from professionals experienced in digital media and entertainment law. Legal experts can provide guidance specific to your situation and help you navigate legal complexities while ensuring compliance with YouTube's policies. Remember that legal advice can be invaluable in protecting your channel and avoiding potential legal pitfalls.

Joining Creator Communities and Networks

Engaging with creator communities and joining reputable YouTube networks can provide valuable support and guidance in understanding and navigating YouTube's policies. These communities offer forums, workshops, and resources that can help you stay informed about policy updates and best practices. Collaborating with fellow creators and leveraging the collective knowledge and experiences of a community can be instrumental in growing your channel while maintaining compliance with YouTube's policies.

As a YouTube creator aiming to make millions, it is essential to keep up with YouTube's policies and guidelines. By understanding and adhering to these policies, you can create a safe and compliant environment for your viewers, avoid legal issues, and maximize your revenue potential. Regularly educate yourself on the latest policy updates through the YouTube Help Center, Creator Insider, and YouTube News. By staying informed and navigating

YouTube's policies effectively, you can build a successful and sustainable YouTube channel.

Chapter 40

Understanding YouTube Algorithm Updates

YouTube is a powerhouse in the online world, with millions of content creators vying for attention and success on the platform. As a creator, it is essential to understand the YouTube algorithm and its updates to maximize your visibility, reach, and ultimately, your earning potential. In this chapter, we will delve deep into the intricacies of the YouTube algorithm, its updates, and how you can adapt your strategies to stay ahead of the game.

The YouTube Algorithm: A Brief Overview

The YouTube algorithm is a complex system that determines which videos appear on users' homepages, search results, and recommendations. Its primary goal is to serve relevant and engaging content to each viewer based on their interests, search history, and viewing patterns. YouTube's algorithm considers various factors when ranking videos, including watch time, engagement, video quality, and user satisfaction.

Understanding YouTube Algorithm Updates

YouTube continuously updates its algorithm to improve the user experience and maintain the platform's integrity. These updates are rolled out periodically and can have a significant impact on video performance and discoverability. By staying informed about these updates, you can adapt your content and strategies accordingly to maintain or boost your channel's visibility. Let's explore some of the notable algorithm updates that have taken place in recent times.

Quality Content and User Satisfaction

YouTube's algorithm increasingly prioritizes quality content and user satisfaction. In the past, videos with click bait titles and thumbnails could manipulate the algorithm and garner views. However, recent updates have focused on rewarding videos that genuinely engage and satisfy viewers. This shift emphasizes the importance of creating high-quality content that provides value, entertains, educates, or solves a problem for your target audience.

To ensure user satisfaction, pay attention to the following factors:

a) Watch Time: YouTube values videos that keep viewers engaged for longer durations. Aim to create compelling content that captivates your audience's attention and encourages them to watch until the end.

b) Average View Duration: This metric measures the average length of time viewers watch your videos. Create engaging intros, concise yet informative content, and strong call-to-actions to improve your average view duration.

c) Audience Retention: YouTube analyzes how much of your video viewers watch before they drop off. Identify patterns where viewers tend to lose interest and make adjustments to maintain their attention throughout the video.

Video Metadata and Optimization

YouTube algorithm updates also focus on video metadata and optimization techniques. Metadata includes your video title, description, tags, and closed captions. Optimizing these elements correctly can significantly impact your video's discoverability and ranking. Here are some tips:

a) Title: Craft attention-grabbing and concise titles that accurately reflect your video's content. Incorporate relevant keywords to enhance search visibility.

b) Description: Write informative and keyword-rich descriptions that provide context and value to your video. Include timestamps, links to relevant resources, and a compelling call-to-action.

c) Tags: Select relevant tags that describe your video's topic, target audience, and key themes. Use both broad and specific tags to increase the chances of appearing in relevant searches.

d) Closed Captions: Transcribe and add closed captions to your videos. This improves accessibility and allows YouTube to index your content more accurately.

Engagement and Interaction

YouTube encourages meaningful interactions between creators and viewers. The algorithm considers engagement metrics such as likes, dislikes, comments, and shares when ranking videos. Here's how you can boost engagement on your channel:

a) Encourage Interaction: Prompt viewers to like, comment, share, and subscribe to your channel through clear calls-to-action. To attract a devoted audience, respond to comments and promote a sense of community.

b) Comments and Moderation: Encourage constructive comments and engage with your viewers' feedback. Moderating comments and removing spam or offensive content helps maintain a positive environment.

c) Video Responses: Create video responses or follow-ups to popular videos in your niche. This strategy can help increase exposure and collaboration opportunities.

Click-Through Rate (CTR)

YouTube's algorithm considers the click-through rate (CTR), which measures the number of times your video is clicked in relation to its impressions. A higher CTR indicates that your video's title, thumbnail, and metadata are compelling and relevant to users.

To optimize your CTR

Create visually appealing thumbnails that accurately represent your video's content. Use clear, high-resolution images, bold text, and contrasting colors to grab attention. Experiment with different thumbnail designs and titles to identify what resonates best with your audience. Split-testing can help you determine the most effective combinations.

Trending Topics and Freshness

YouTube aims to promote timely and relevant content to its users. Videos covering trending topics or current events often receive a boost in visibility. Stay updated with the latest trends and leverage them to create timely content. Additionally, uploading videos regularly signals to the algorithm that your channel is active and engaging.

Mobile Optimization and Responsiveness

In today's digital landscape, mobile devices play a significant role in video consumption. YouTube recognizes this trend and prioritizes mobile-optimized content in its algorithm updates. With more users accessing YouTube on smartphones and tablets, it's crucial to ensure that your videos are mobile-friendly and provide an excellent user experience across different devices.

a) **Responsive Design:** Create video content that adapts seamlessly to various screen sizes. Ensure that your thumbnails, titles, and video formatting are optimized for mobile viewing.

b) **Shorter Video Length:** Mobile users often prefer shorter videos due to limited attention spans and on-the-go viewing habits. Consider creating concise, impactful videos that deliver value within a shorter timeframe.

c) **Vertical Video:** Vertical video format is gaining popularity, especially on mobile platforms like Instagram and TikTok. Experiment with vertical videos to cater to the preferences of mobile users and potentially boost engagement.

Viewer Feedback and Watch Patterns

YouTube values viewer feedback and utilizes it to refine the algorithm and provide a personalized user experience. By analyzing viewer watch patterns, interactions, and feedback, YouTube can better understand user preferences and deliver content that aligns with their interests. As a content creator, you can leverage this aspect of the algorithm to optimize your videos for viewer satisfaction.

a) **Analytics and Insights:** Utilize YouTube's analytics tools to gain insights into your viewers' behavior. Analyze metrics like audience retention, traffic sources, and demographics to understand your audience's preferences and tailor your content accordingly.

b) **Viewer Surveys and Polls:** Engage directly with your audience by conducting surveys or polls within your videos or through community posts. This feedback can help you gather valuable insights and adjust your content strategy to better meet your viewers' expectations.

c) Test and Iterate: Continuously experiment with different video formats, topics, and styles based on viewer feedback and watch patterns. Analyze the performance of your videos and make data-driven decisions to improve engagement and satisfaction.

By understanding and leveraging viewer feedback and watch patterns, you can align your content strategy with the preferences of your audience, leading to increased engagement, retention, and overall success on YouTube.

Understanding the YouTube algorithm and its updates is crucial for success as a content creator. By focusing on creating high-quality, engaging content, optimizing video metadata, encouraging audience interaction, improving CTR, and staying updated with trending topics, you can enhance your chances of appearing in users' recommendations, search results, and homepages. Remember, the YouTube algorithm is continually evolving, so it's essential to adapt your strategies and techniques accordingly. Stay informed, experiment, and keep refining your content to maximize your visibility and reach millions on YouTube.

Remember, mastering the YouTube algorithm is an ongoing process, and it requires constant monitoring, analyzing, and adapting. By staying proactive and implementing the strategies outlined in this chapter, you'll be well-equipped to navigate the YouTube ecosystem and make millions from your YouTube channel.

Chapter 41

How Much YouTube Pay for ONE Million views?

YOUTUBE HAS EMERGED AS a powerful platform for content creators to showcase their talent, share knowledge, and entertain audiences worldwide. With the increasing popularity of YouTube, many individuals aspire to become successful YouTubers and earn a steady income from their channels. In this article, we will delve into the fascinating world of YouTuber earnings, exploring the factors that influence their monthly income and uncovering the potential earnings at various subscriber milestones.

Understanding the Revenue Sources on YouTube

To comprehend how YouTubers earn money, it is essential to understand the revenue sources available on the platform. The primary sources of income for YouTubers include ads, sponsorships, merchandise sales, channel memberships, Super Chat, and YouTube Premium revenue. However, for the purpose of this article, we will primarily focus on ad revenue, as it forms a significant portion of a YouTuber's monthly earnings.

The First Milestone: 1000 Subscribers

When a YouTuber reaches 1000 subscribers and accumulates 4000 watch hours within the past 12 months, they become eligible to apply for the YouTube Partner Program (YPP). Once accepted into the program, YouTubers can monetize their content through ads, subscriptions, and channel memberships. However, it's important to note that the earnings at this stage are relatively modest, and the primary focus should be on building an engaged audience and consistently producing high-quality content.

10,000 Subscribers: A Significant Achievement

Reaching 10,000 subscribers marks a significant milestone in a YouTuber's journey. At this point, they have gained some traction and can potentially earn a more substantial income. The earnings for YouTubers with 10,000 subscribers can vary widely, depending on factors such as video views, engagement, niche, and ad types. According to reports, YouTubers can earn anywhere from $1 to $10 per 1000 views, which translates to an average monthly income of $100 to $1000 with 100,000 monthly views.

100,000 Subscribers: Unlocking Greater Earnings

With 100,000 subscribers, a YouTuber enters the league of established creators with a dedicated fan base. At this stage, they can expect a significant boost in their earnings compared to earlier milestones. The ad revenue increases, and they also gain access to additional monetization features such as channel memberships and Super Chat. On average, a YouTuber with 100,000 subscribers can earn between $500 and $5000 per month, depending on various factors such as niche, engagement, and ad revenue fluctuations.

1 Million Subscribers: The Earning Potential is High

Reaching the coveted 1 million subscriber mark unlocks a whole new level of earning potential for YouTubers. At this stage, they have established themselves as influential creators and can attract high-paying sponsorships and brand collaborations. The income of YouTubers with 1 million subscribers varies significantly, ranging from $5000 to $50,000 per month or even more. Successful YouTubers can diversify their revenue streams by launching merchandise, creating online courses, or engaging in affiliate marketing.

10 Million Subscribers: The Elite Club

YouTubers who achieve the remarkable feat of amassing 10 million subscribers are part of an elite club. They enjoy immense popularity and have the potential to earn staggering amounts of money. At this stage, YouTubers can earn substantial revenue from ad placements, brand partnerships, sponsored content, and endorsements. Their monthly income can easily surpass six figures, ranging from $50,000 to well over $100,000, depending on their niche, engagement rate, and business ventures.

Beyond Subscribers: Diversifying Income Streams

While the number of subscribers plays a significant role in a YouTuber's earnings, it is crucial to explore additional avenues for generating income. Successful YouTubers often diversify their revenue streams to reduce reliance on ad revenue alone. They may create and sell digital products such as e-books or online courses, offer personalized services, engage in affiliate marketing, or establish their brand through merchandise sales. By diversifying their income streams, YouTubers can create more stability and maximize their earning potential.

Factors Influencing YouTube Earnings

Various factors influence a YouTuber's monthly earnings. These factors include ad revenue fluctuations, viewer demographics, viewer engagement, video length, ad placement, viewer location, and seasonality. Advertisers may pay different rates based on the type of content or audience demographics, which can impact a YouTuber's earnings significantly. Additionally, a YouTuber's engagement rate, the number of likes, comments, and shares on their videos, plays a crucial role in attracting high-paying brand collaborations and sponsorships.

Earning money on YouTube is an exciting prospect for content creators, but it requires dedication, perseverance, and a deep understanding of the platform's dynamics. While the income potential varies greatly based on factors like subscriber count, engagement, and niche, it is clear that YouTube offers a viable opportunity for individuals to turn their passion into a lucrative profession. Whether you're just starting or aiming for millions of subscribers, consistency, creativity, and building a genuine connection with your audience remain the key ingredients for success on YouTube.

Chapter 42

The Final Stretch: Wishing You Millions on Your YouTube Journey

Congratulations! You've reached the final chapter of "How to Make Millions from YouTube." We hope this book has provided you with invaluable insights and strategies to pave your path towards YouTube success and financial abundance. As you embark on your journey to make millions, we want to leave you with a heartfelt wish for your continued prosperity.

First and foremost, we wish you unwavering determination and perseverance. Building a million-dollar empire on YouTube requires a steadfast commitment to excellence. Stay focused on creating exceptional content, nurturing your audience, and constantly refining your craft. Let your unwavering drive fuel your pursuit of success, even when faced with obstacles.

Secondly, we wish you adaptability and innovation. The YouTube landscape is ever-evolving, with new trends, algorithms, and technologies shaping the industry. Embrace change, stay informed, and be open to exploring innovative strategies. Your ability to adapt and innovate will be instrumental in staying ahead of the curve and capitalizing on emerging opportunities.

Additionally, we wish you a supportive network and collaborative spirit. Surround yourself with like-minded creators, mentors, and advocates who inspire and uplift you. Seek out communities and partnerships where you can exchange knowledge, share experiences, and propel each other's growth. Together, you can forge new paths and amplify your collective impact.

Lastly, we wish you fulfillment and happiness on your journey. While financial success is undoubtedly a significant aspect, remember to find joy in the creative process, the connections you make with your audience, and the positive impact you have on their lives. Strive for a balanced and fulfilling YouTube career that brings you both financial rewards and personal satisfaction.

Recapping our journey together, we started by laying the groundwork for your YouTube success, exploring monetization strategies, expanding your reach, and mastering advanced techniques. We delved into various revenue streams, honed your content strategy, and equipped you with the tools to overcome challenges along the way. We drew inspiration from the success stories of thriving YouTubers and extracted valuable lessons from their experiences.

As you conclude this book, take a moment to reflect on the knowledge you've acquired and the progress you've made. Let that reflection fuel your ambition and propel you towards your million-dollar goals.

Thank you for joining us on this transformative exploration, and we sincerely hope that "How to Make Millions from YouTube" has empowered you to unlock your full potential and create a prosperous future on the platform. Now, armed with the knowledge and strategies shared, it's time for you to step into the spotlight and make your mark.

Wishing you boundless success, abundant wealth, and an extraordinary journey ahead. May your YouTube endeavors lead you to the millions you aspire to, and may every video be a stepping stone towards financial freedom.

Farewell, and may your YouTube dreams become a reality.

About the Author

Hamza Munir Bhatti is a renowned entrepreneur, industrialist, and educationist who has made significant contributions in various sectors internationally. He has received numerous accolades and recognition for his relentless services and achievements.

Awarded the prestigious "Son of Lahore" title by the President of Pakistan under the flagship of Lahore Chamber of Commerce, Hamza Munir Bhatti's dedication and commitment to both the industrial and educational sectors have been acknowledged. His efforts have not only brought global recognition but have also played a vital role in the growth of these sectors. As the acclaimed "Youngest Entrepreneur," featured in Manager Today Magazine, Hamza Munir Bhatti has demonstrated his exceptional abilities in the industrial sector on an international level.

Hamza Munir Bhatti has been honoured as one of the "100 Best Performing CEOs" at the CEO Summit Asia 2015. His visionary leadership and strategic management skills have led to the remarkable success of Mr. Denim, making it one of the largest Denim Jeans Exporters worldwide. By collaborating with leading international brands of United States and Europe, Hamza Munir Bhatti has revolutionized the textile industry and expanded its reach across the globe.

Hamza Munir Bhatti is also the founder of Mega News Tv , The Fastest growing Digital news website , with its website www.meganews.tv, has garnered a massive following of over 1 million within a year from all over the world on various digital platforms.

In the education sector, Hamza Munir Bhatti has established two prestigious institutions, Lords Law College and Lords College of Pharmacy. These institutions have gained international recognition through collaborations in research work within the legal and pharmaceutical industries. Hamza Munir Bhatti's commitment to education and his efforts in fostering international collaborations showcase his dedication to knowledge and innovation.

With his profound experience and invaluable contributions across multiple sectors, Hamza Munir Bhatti is now venturing into writing. He is set to release upcoming books in the business, media, and education sectors, sharing his expertise and insights garnered from his successful career. Hamza Munir Bhatti's books are expected to offer valuable guidance and inspiration to the youth and aspiring entrepreneurs, professionals, and individuals seeking knowledge in these domains.